Michelle Glogovac's superpower is connection. In her latest book, *How to Get on Podcasts,* she shares stories to inspire, motivate, and educate others through the power of podcast interviews. Her insights and wisdom will help you ignite that same connection magic to tell your story through this powerful medium.

—**Emma Isaacs**, founder, Business Chicks

Michelle Glogovac knows how to connect people, build lasting relationships, and help you share your story with the world. *How to Get on Podcasts* imparts all of her podcast wisdom and is the absolute guidebook that all business leaders and nonprofit organizations should be referring to.

—**Nisha Anand**, CEO, Dream.Org

Why are we so afraid to tell our stories? Because we don't know how. Michelle Glogovac is ensuring that readers become ultimate storytellers. *How to Get on Podcasts* empowers you to tell your story in a way that showcases your expertise and elevates your business. This book is a must-read.

—**Allyson Byrd**, Oracle & Conscious Voice Alchemist

# Praise for *How to Get on Podcasts*

Michelle Glogovac's warmth, compassion, inquisitive nature, an
ful demeanor are evident throughout her book. Told like advice
good friend, *How to Get on Podcasts* will become the ultimate so
anyone looking to grow an audience. A fabulous and fun read
mover and shaker in the podcast space. I'll be recommending th
and left!

—**Zibby Owens**, host of *Moms Don't Have Time to Re*

Every author in America needs this book!

—**Leigh Stein**, author of

Got a story? Ready to share it? Michelle Glogovac delivers a
to help you go from wanting to be a podcast guest to getting
regularly.

—**Meaghan B Murphy**, author of *Your Fully Ch*

*How to Get on Podcasts* is a valuable read filled with lesson
gold. A true guide for those wanting to share their story mo
on podcasts. Michelle Glogovac does an excellent job of sho
how to get booked on the winning podcasts, plus share our
knowledge in a way that will have impact. *How to Get on P*
winner!

—**Kara Goldin**, founder and former CEO
author of *WSJ* bestseller
host of *The Kara*

# HOW TO GET ON
# PODCASTS

# HOW TO GET ON
# PODCASTS

CULTIVATE YOUR FOLLOWING, STRENGTHEN
YOUR MESSAGE, AND GROW AS A THOUGHT
LEADER THROUGH PODCAST GUESTING

## MICHELLE L. GLOGOVAC
### THE PODCAST MATCHMAKER™

NEW YORK   CHICAGO   SAN FRANCISCO   ATHENS   LONDON
MADRID   MEXICO CITY   MILAN   NEW DELHI
SINGAPORE   SYDNEY   TORONTO

1 2 3 4 5 6 7 8 9   LCR   28 27 26 25 24 23

ISBN       978-1-265-54362-4
MHID          1-265-54362-3

e-ISBN   978-1-265-54980-0
e-MHID      1-265-54980-X

This publication is designed to provide accurate and authoritative information in regard to the subject matter covered. It is sold with the understanding that neither the author nor the publisher is engaged in rendering legal, accounting, securities trading, or other professional services. If legal advice or other expert assistance is required, the services of a competent professional person should be sought.

—*From a Declaration of Principles Jointly Adopted by a Committee of the American Bar Association and a Committee of Publishers and Associations*

McGraw Hill books are available at special quantity discounts to use as premiums and sales promotions or for use in corporate training programs. To contact a representative, please visit the Contact Us pages at www.mhprofessional.com.

McGraw Hill is committed to making our products accessible to all learners. To learn more about the available support and accommodations we offer, please contact us at accessibility@mheducation.com. We also participate in the Access Text Network (www.accesstext.org), and ATN members may submit requests through ATN.

*For Ted . . .*
You supported me as I found
my voice over the years . . .
and then loved me even more.

*For Declan and Katharine . . .*
May you always use your voice for good,
share your story, and listen to the stories of others.
You have the power to change the world,
and I will always believe in you.

# CONTENTS

# INTRODUCTION

I n my twenties not only did I travel a lot for work, but I also moved around the country quite a bit. I lived in Paradise, Santa Barbara, Santa Maria, Los Angeles, Houston, Chicago, and San Jose (in that order!), all before I was 27 years old and in just a matter of 9 years. When I moved to each new city, I might have known one or two people, but I always had a goal of making new friends. When I became a mom, I wanted to make mom friends so that my kids would also have some friends to play with at the park and I would have other moms to talk with—hey, no one wants to only have tiny humans to chat with all day! Now that I'm in my forties, I can proudly say I have friends in every place I've ever lived, I have a great group of mom friends, and I've made other types of friends along the way. I'm an entertainer at heart. I love nothing more than hosting happy hours at my home with friends, creating a themed dinner menu, or planning an Oktoberfest party. But there's something that makes a BBQ or wine-tasting evening more fun . . . friends. Finding new friends and creating these dinner parties or backyard movie nights is essentially like finding the right podcast to be interviewed on. You have to find the right people that connect with you and vice versa to ensure your time together is not only memorable but actually fun and enjoyable.

I've never been one to shy away from letting people know I like them and would like to be their friend. I now understand that this behavior per se is kind of rare (and might come off as odd), but I think it's a great way to engage. I'm absolutely not kidding when I tell you that I will actually say out loud that I like you, and I have a great example to back it up. I went to Sir Richard Branson's home on Necker Island in 2022 with a group of 30 women from around the world. I had been invited as a part of the Business Chicks network to attend a seven day retreat filled with guest speakers, yoga, water excursions, and time to reflect. I did my homework beforehand and read one of Richard's books (yes, we are on a first-name basis!), and I also paid close attention to the speakers who presented to us. When I had dinner with Richard, I told him I knew his life story already; therefore, I felt like I knew him and that we were already friends. He chuckled and agreed (he's kind like that) and then asked about me so that he could reciprocate my feelings. One of the presenters during the week was Cathy Burke. Cathy is a speaker, author and global change maker who was the CEO of The Hunger Project for 20 years. She spoke in the most calming manner and had fantastic stories to share which included how she worked with women in South Asia and Africa to truly change their mindsets and recognize that they were in more control of their future than they thought. Her presentations included how we all have more power to make the same changes in our own lives. I went up to her on the first day (after having cried my eyes out because it had been all kinds of emotional) and told her I liked her. This again brought on a chuckle because people don't normally do this, and as our time during the week progressed, she autographed her book for me and wrote, "I like you too." I share these stories with you because I think that being vulnerable and honest are two of the most human traits you can show another person. If you're genuine and share yourself, you're going to succeed in everything you do, including podcast guesting.

I've taken inventory of myself and what I have to offer, so I know what I look for in a new friend. I know what makes me the person I am and what kind of friend I can be. For starters, I'm dependable, a go-getter, a great listener, and outspoken, and I will stand up for what is right and what I believe in. I openly share this about myself, and it's what draws those who want to be my friend to me. In all my podcast interviews and on my own show, *My Simplified Life*, I share freely and honestly with listeners. I offer up my experience and how I got to where I am today, along with what frightens me and what my hopes and dreams are for my children. Not only do I offer my personal experiences, but I share my knowledge as much as possible. You're going to discover that this is the utter truth as you read this book and find that I didn't leave a single detail out when it comes to podcast guesting . . . I promise!

As we go through different stages in life, we encounter and need different types of friends. You know what I'm talking about—you have friends who are work friends, friends that you've known since you were a child, college friends, parent friends, neighbor friends, casual friends, the friend you can call night or day for a shoulder to cry on or to borrow $100. Just as there are different types of friends, there are different topics that we can speak on . . . more on this as you keep reading! Each type of friendship can represent a speaking topic category. Let me explain.

You've got a friend that you've known since kindergarten—someone you can call randomly and pick up right where you left off. This is your friend that is like your "personal story." This friend knows what your life has been like, knows your history, and has a history with you. For me, that friend is Lisa, whom I've known since before kindergarten.

In your work life you might have a business bestie or work spouse. This is someone you can openly share financial details with, client struggles, and the pressure you're feeling at any given moment. This friend listens to you and also celebrates with you. This is your "business-story" friend. My business-story friend is my dear friend Keren who has been my business BFF and confidant since I launched my business and has seen the pivots, challenges, and finally the success.

If you have kids and they play sports or you've joined the PTA and made new friends who are going through the same parenting moments that you are currently enduring, then we will call these your "timely-and-relevant" friends (hey, Allison!). They're friends who get you in the here and now, just like the trending news on X (formerly known as Twitter).

We all have neighbors, but there are the ones you just click with. They're the ones who love your street and show pride in their home, who attend the neighborhood watch meeting and want the same things you do for your neighborhood. These are your "signature-method-and-framework" friends. You have a common goal in mind and want to ensure that the neighborhood thrives in the same way . . . this is a perfect description of my neighbor and friend Stephanie (you shouldn't have escaped to the beach!).

Next, we have the friend who is always there for happy hour. This is the friend you can depend on to be present for every party you throw, no matter what the theme is. This is the friend who might just show up on a Friday evening with a bottle of wine knowing that he or she is always welcome at your home and vice versa. These friends are your "experiences" friends because they experience life and fun with you. For me, that's my happy hour crew, which includes Sara, Cindy, and Jill.

Last, but not least, are your friends that you work with. These are your teammates, your coworkers, your industry professionals, and they are your "skill" friends. They get what it takes to do what you do because they're knee-deep in the trenches with you. My skill friends include Michelle (my fellow MG), Tonya, and Jody. They are all publicists who understand what I do and what it takes to get our jobs done.

Notice that I've given each of these types of friends a certain category in quotes. In Chapter 1, we are going to talk about speaking topic categories and the light bulb is going to go off! You're going to think of your topics as types of friends who reflect specific parts of your life. You know them so well and have made such incredible memories, so that it's easy to talk about them and share your experiences with others.

# THIS IS YOUR TOOLBOX FOR EVERYTHING

As you're going to quickly discover, I am a firm believer in sharing what you know so that others may learn from you. I'm a big fan of hearing personal stories and of sharing my own in the hope that it might just help someone going through the same thing. I shared my story of having a pulmonary embolism and my fear of death while in the hospital. Not only did people reach out to say they have the same fear, but they thanked me for saying what they've been afraid of saying. In addition to that, I had people around the country reaching out to say they recently also had a pulmonary embolism and were looking for answers. Sharing your experiences and stories with the world creates a connection with others. I want this book to be YOUR answer on how to get your message, story, cause, experience out for the world to hear and to further connect with people you wouldn't otherwise meet.

The amount of information I'm sharing with you in these pages is an education that has taken me years to learn. If you were to search for books on the topics I've included, you'd need to read at least six separate books to find all the information that is right here in your hands. I want you to take your time reading this book. Do the exercises, come back to the interview tips before you record your first one, make sure you're repurposing your interviews to maximize their visibility, and find ways to increase your marketing that you hadn't thought of before. You'll learn about what public relations is, dive into the podcasting landscape, and find out what hosts are working on through every stage of the process, how to be a great guest, how to utilize your interviews over and over for content, and much more. I'm offering you a complete 360-degree view of what podcast interviews can do for you and what the podcasting industry is about.

Let's start with some definitions.

# WHAT IS PUBLIC RELATIONS?

Public relations, or PR, is the management and distribution of information about an individual or a company to the public. The purpose is to influence how the world sees you and to ensure you're seen in a good light . . . no bad press here! PR can be in the form of a newspaper or magazine interview, a contribution to an article, a press release, a podcast interview—the list is long. When hiring a publicist, you'll work with an individual or agency on your messaging and how you present yourself to the public, and you might also create a crisis communication plan so that you're prepared when something goes wrong. Social media, internal communications, and community relations also fall under the PR umbrella.

Podcast interviews are PR because you're pitching yourself to be interviewed by a podcast host, the interview will be distributed to the public, and you're selecting the way you want to be represented by offering the specific topics or story you're speaking on. You're working on growing media attention with a podcast and building your reputation in your industry. This is exactly what PR is defined as.

# TWO TYPES OF PR: REACTIVE AND PROACTIVE

My goal in this book is to give you all the intel you need to fully understand the podcasting industry and to be armed with enough information to make you slightly dangerous. Aside from the varying categories of PR, there are two types of PR: reactive and proactive.

Reactive PR is when you discover an opportunity from the media. A journalist is already working on a story and is looking for sources . . . you fit the bill. You "react" by reaching out to the journalist (or host), introducing yourself and offering reasons why you're a great fit for the story. There are a number of websites and emails you can subscribe to in order to discover these opportunities, such as HARO (help a reporter out) or Qwoted.

Proactive PR, on the other hand, is when you are looking for media opportunities and create the story for the journalist. You're pitching your story, message, topics, or news to journalists, podcast hosts, and other outlets. You are reaching out to them with your story idea and telling them why you think it's newsworthy. The journalist or host likes it and gets the green light from the editor or producer to move forward with an interview with you. Podcast pitching falls into the proactive category. These are stories or topics that weren't already in the works ... YOU created them.

## HOSTING A PODCAST VERSUS BEING A PODCAST GUEST

There's a big difference in hosting your own podcast and being a guest on someone else's show. I could probably write another book just on this topic! Hosting a show can and is great for a business's brand because it offers value to their consumers. Trader Joe's has a show called *Inside Trader Joe's*, which not only gives listeners (aka shoppers) a glimpse at what they have going on in their stores, but also offers an education on things such as what a tasting panel is or what private label means. It's not a must-have, but it is another way for Trader Joe's to get their brand in front of potential customers.

Business branded podcasts are a great way for companies to connect with an audience, but I'm a bigger fan of having a company's team members share their stories as podcast guests. There's a potential to reach a greater number of listeners and allow people to get to know the actual humans in your organization. I have worked for a number of years with Van Jones's nonprofit, Dream.Org. I pitch six of their team members to share their journeys, knowledge, and the "why" behind why they're a part of Dream.Org's mission. In six months, we reached over 300,000 podcast listeners. One of the team members said he had forged new relationships with hosts and listeners, new collaborations and ways of doing their work, and hosts who heard him on podcast interviews asking to speak with him. The ripple effect of having a company's team members share their story is most often much more far-reaching than a business's branded podcast.

## ISN'T PITCHING SOMETHING IN BASEBALL?

In baseball, the ball is pitched to the batter to hit. In PR, pitching is basically the same thing, but a story idea replaces the ball. You are sending that story to an outlet in the hope that the people there like it enough to strike a home run and publish it. A pitch in PR, and more specifically to podcasts, is the email you are going to send to the host that explains why you should be interviewed on the person's show. Your pitch is going to include all the information necessary to get a host to say yes. It's going to highlight you in a variety of ways, but at the same time it's going to be all about the host and the host's show. Don't worry about the "how" behind doing this right in this moment because I'm giving you step-by-step instructions very shortly!

## DO I NEED SOCIAL MEDIA OR A WEBSITE BEFORE I PITCH MYSELF?

The short answer . . . YES! You've started reading this book, and you are ready to get your voice out into the world. BUT before we start, let's talk about a couple of things you should have set up in place before you even get to Chapter 1, create your media kit, or even send that first pitch.

Do you have a website? I'm hoping the answer is yes, because if it isn't, you need to get one set up. I promise you it doesn't have to be fancy, so please keep reading! At the bare minimum, you should purchase a website domain and have a home page that shares who you are, a page that describes what you do, a media/press page (don't worry—we are going to cover that in Chapter 8), and a way for people to contact you. I have had some clients come to me with just a one-page website that covers all this, and that's fine to begin with. Just make sure that you understand you will be adding to your website and will want a place for blog posts and (as noted above) a media/press page—and you'll want all of it aligned with your brand (your fonts, colors, and logo). If you aren't sure about what domain name to go with, start with your name. I recommend that people own their own name domain. You can redirect your domain name to your business website or just park it, but it's a great must-have.

When it comes to social media, you need it. If you don't have a social media presence, start those accounts! It's not important that you have a huge following to land podcast interviews. What is important is that someone can find you on social media and that you have a platform where you can share your podcast interviews with your followers. Which social media platforms you should be on will depend on where your ideal/target audience hangs out. Your choices include Instagram (highly recommended because podcasters are there), Facebook, X, LinkedIn, Pinterest, and TikTok. By curating content for social media, you're also going to elevate your brand and thought leadership.

Where is your audience hanging out? It might surprise a lot of people, but Pinterest is not just a platform for moms making crafts and looking for dinner inspo. There are a ton of references for entrepreneurs, podcasters, and more. Pinterest is a great tool to drive traffic to your website. I mention all of this because I want you to look at the bigger picture when it comes to social media. Pinterest is technically a visual search engine, but it's also known as an image-based social media network . . . so it counts! A lot of people disregard the power of X as well, but that little blue bird has some incredibly supportive people who make great connections using it, including journalists and podcast hosts. I discuss in more detail the trials and tribulations of X in Chapter 7, but for now, know that you want a platform where there's great networking and journalists like to hang out.

Before you start rolling your eyes or stressing out over having to create content for all these platforms, I want to let you in on a little secret. The podcast interviews you are going to land are going to provide you with a TON of content. You simply need to show up on these platforms and engage with others. Let them know you exist and want to make new friends! It's truly as simple as that. We are going to create plug-and-play material so that you will be able to show up in a simple way that doesn't cause you stress!

## EMAIL LIST

Have you already created an email list? If not, now is the time. Hey, I get it . . . I started a blog five years before launching my business, and never once did I collect any email addresses, nor did I understand the importance of collecting them. I kick myself for not starting earlier, but you can't go back in time. The people who give you their email address in order to follow you, in exchange for your freebies (we'll cover that in Chapter 5!), and want to consume more of your content are the ones who are truly your audience, potential clients, fans, community, and everything you want followers to be.

If you haven't signed up for an email subscription service, let's take care of that. You can check out Flodesk (it's what I use!) or Substack, Mailchimp, HubSpot, ActiveCampaign, Constant Contact, or any of the other email marketing platforms that are available. Get your account set up so that you can start collecting those email addresses and growing your community! This is going to be a must-have because you want to have a place to collect email addresses when you offer up your call to action (we discuss this in Chapter 5) at the end of every podcast interview.

## CREATING AND ELEVATING YOUR PERSONAL BRAND

Your personal brand is your intentional way of representing yourself. It's positioning yourself as an authority in your industry, elevating your credibility, advancing your career, increasing your circle of influence, and having a greater impact on what you stand for. A personal brand is simply showing the world who you are and what you're about. It's in no way pompous or showy if you do it the right way. Think of it as being informational for those who don't know you.

You are your personal brand, but are you elevating yourself properly? More and more, we are hearing about how you are your own brand, but what does that mean or even look like? For decades if you had a corporate job (which I did for 20 years), you were simply an extension of the company's brand. Your banner on your LinkedIn profile probably included the company logo, and you were marketing on the company's behalf, when in reality, you should have been promoting yourself more.

As we've seen with the "Great Resignation," people suddenly realized that they hadn't been promoting themselves or their beliefs or expertise enough. They also realized that when it comes to a corporate job, there isn't much loyalty on the part of the company . . . so why are you being so loyal? Ah, this is the million dollar question these days! Having and promoting your personal brand isn't being disloyal to your company if you have a corporate job. It's simply amplifying your talents and expertise and creating awareness around who you are and what you know . . . perfect if you find yourself in a situation where you are looking for a new job or a promotion!

For starters, as noted above, you should own the domain of your name. Even if you aren't quite sure what to do with it, you should at least purchase it and be the owner of your name domain. I bought my name domain many years ago and currently have it redirected to my agency website. As I continue to expand my presence, I'll be changing my personal website to offer visitors a glimpse into who I am, where I've been, what my achievements are, and more. I'll include all the pieces of a regular website (about me, media/press page, contact info), but they'll be specifically for me, not my business (although there will be info on my agency with a link to the website, of course!). This is a part of my personal brand.

Defining your personal brand allows you to show your uniqueness and build your reputation the way you want. This is where podcast interviews come into play. They're a perfect way for you to showcase and share your knowledge and expertise, as well as focus on the subject matter that you want to be known as the expert on. It doesn't matter if you are still in the middle of a corporate job, whether you plan on staying or have other goals or aspirations that you'd like to achieve. It's OK to put yourself in the spotlight by being a podcast guest and sharing what you know.

We can look at it from two different angles, one being that at some point in your life you won't still be working at the company you are at now. At some time, you will retire, and from those that I know who are enjoying retirement, they're still wanting to keep busy and share the knowledge they've acquired after working for so many years. What if you've already laid the foundation for people to recognize all your knowledge and experience and have the opportunity to continue sharing it on podcast shows? The second angle we should consider is that companies change. They're bought; they have layoffs; they go public. This could land you in a number of new positions that you're not currently in. If you've taken the time to create your personal brand and focus on you and not only the company you've worked for, then the rest of the world already knows who you are, and it increases your chance of discovering your next big adventure.

Who am I to suggest having a fallback plan? I was laid off twice. I worked for a company for a decade, and it was honestly the best company in the industry I worked in. When I was laid off, I felt like any other competitor would certainly be a step down. I accepted a position with another company that was a slight competitor, but it was honest and trustworthy, which was high on my priority list for whatever company I went to work for next. Of course, this next company was purchased by a larger conglomerate, and as one of the last in, I was one of the first out. I had been focused for almost two decades on the companies I worked for and the industry I was in. I had never focused on myself or promoting myself in any kind of way. What people knew about me was my loyalty to two Fortune 100 corporations, my work ethic in ensuring I was always there for my clients, my sales abilities, and how freaking organized I was (I could upsell like it was no one's business while remembering birthdays and anniversaries), along with having the skills to be on national and regional boards creating new networking opportunities for others in the industry.

In a way, that was my personal brand, but it wasn't done in a purposeful manner. I was simply doing my job and then some. Instead, I should have focused on what it was like to be a very young 21-year-old and find myself in a position of being responsible for the financials of a base with a monthly income in the millions or being the Fortune 50's youngest salesperson to ever be hired and exceed sales goals by over 200 percent. As time went on, I could have shared what it was like to go back to school while working or being a full-time working mom with two under two. While I had a budding social media presence, I had no focus on building a personal brand for myself or focusing on building myself up as an individual.

Today, my personal brand encompasses not only what I do in my business and my love for all things podcasting, but also my passion to make the world a better place, such as volunteering with various nonprofits, being involved with my local government, and raising money for my children's school . . . it shows that I'm involved, action-oriented, and passionate and will "fight like a mother," as Shannon Watts, founder of Moms Demand Action says. My personal brand also ties together how my professional experience helps my personal causes and vice versa. I'm able to show the world who I am, what I'm an expert on, what I believe in, and what my experience entails.

## WHEN SHOULD YOU START PITCHING YOURSELF AND BEING INTERVIEWED?

You've picked up this book, and you think podcast interviews are your next step. Now you're wondering, when is the right time to pitch yourself and be a podcast guest? The answer is that the right time is yesterday, so start now! As with most things in life, you might not feel ready, but this book is going to get you ready. You're going to be ready in regard to not only pitching yourself and being interview-ready but also knowing how to repurpose your interviews and create amazing marketing content. Not only that, but we'll work on your mindset and get rid of those pesky butterflies that pop up just before speaking!

Sharing your knowledge, story, and voice with the world doesn't need to wait for the perfect moment. Now is the perfect moment! You're already an expert. Your book is about to launch. Your movement is growing. You're ready to run for office. NOW is the time to amplify your voice, because there are people literally waiting to hear from you. That might sound like an exaggeration, but it's not. I have been interviewed hundreds of times, and I've landed thousands of interviews for clients. I can tell you wholeheartedly that not only are people looking for these types of interviews, but the interviews will be met with rave reviews exclaiming how useful and needed they are. Your interview will be no different.

Podcast interviews are all about conversations between two people that you wouldn't otherwise be privy to. I'm a truth teller, so let me admit that I'm the biggest eavesdropper around. I love to hear what others are talking about, and podcast interviews allow for you to eavesdrop on conversations you wouldn't normally be a part of. By being a guest, you're welcoming strangers to eavesdrop and learn from your conversations as well. Let people into your conversation, share your knowledge, and stop making them wait to hear what you have to say . . . or worse, hear it from someone else.

Throughout this book, you're going to discover a new comfort level that allows you to be yourself while sharing your story, your expertise, your opinion, your mission. Now is the time for you to share what you know with the world. Don't wait until next month or next year or when you feel like you just might be a bit more ready. You're about to discover that podcast guesting isn't just great for business and visibility, but that it is extremely fulfilling. When you receive the feedback from a complete stranger telling you how you've helped the person in some way or expressing simple gratitude, you're going to discover a new kind of happiness and fulfillment. This book is going to get you ready to have these conversations . . . and prepare you for a new kind of joy!

# WHAT MAKES ME THE PODCAST MATCHMAKER™?

Growing up I wanted to be an attorney. At age five, I took my dad's briefcase to school instead of a backpack. In fifth grade I said I was going to live on the beach. In high school, I looked at colleges that had a law major as an option. I ended up going to the University of California, Santa Barbara (if you're not familiar with Santa Barbara, please know that it's located along the Pacific coast—wonderful beaches!), and was a law-and-society major. Once in college, I discovered that money was spent very quickly between having to pay for tuition and room and board and having to pay for being the cockswain of the crew team (crew was a rec sport, which meant you had to pay for it), so I had to get a job. Lucky for me, the airport was within walking distance, so I applied and was hired on the spot at the general aviation terminal. Once I graduated, all my friends seemed to be moving back home to live with their parents while looking for a job, but my aviation job offered me a salary and benefits, so I stayed. Almost 20 years later, I found myself still in corporate aviation.

My aviation career lasted so long because I really enjoyed the people I worked with. I knew every single one of my customers in my territory and made the greatest effort possible to get to know them on a personal level. I listened to them when they spoke and understood not only what their business pain points were, but what was going on in their personal lives. Things changed when my children were born. I wanted to do something that was more impactful on the world, and I discovered podcasting.

I had a client ask me to pitch her to podcasts because she knew I understood and liked her work. I had been producing her podcast and had been sharing the content that resonated with me, and I was helping her create content for her show. As they say, the rest is history . . . I found my purpose and my passion. But what makes me THE Podcast Matchmaker? It's my ability not only to decipher what the goals and messaging of my clients are, but to discover the same when it comes to podcast hosts. I don't copy and paste. I don't throw spaghetti at the wall in the hope that a pitch will stick and resonate with someone. I get personal. I share my clients and myself with the hosts, and I let the hosts know that I did some stalking of them as well.

## THIS IS ABOUT RELATIONSHIPS— THERE'S NO ROOM FOR AI

This book is ALL me . . . I didn't use AI, or artificial intelligence, to help me or to come up with ideas for any part of this book, nor do I use AI in my business. As I'm writing, AI is a huge topic of conversation, along with the rising popularity of the app ChatGPT. Individuals and corporations are using AI to create their content, find out personal information to discover the best sales tactics to use for decision makers, write their college essays with, and much more. The other day I saw a post on LinkedIn about how ChatGPT was being used by a PR agency to create speaking topics, write pitches, craft thank you notes, write podcast show notes, and so on. My advice to you is to NOT use AI for any of the exercises you will be doing and to never rely on AI for your speaking topics and certainly not for your pitches.

I'm not against AI per se and think utilizing it once you have content created can potentially be helpful. To create unique speaking topics for yourself, though, you need to have an understanding of what you can speak on, not what an app can spit out. Let's also not forget that we will want unique speaking topics, and chances are that an AI app is going to generate something that someone has already created or spoken on. If you have a signature method or framework, an AI tool is not going to help you stand out by offering up a title that someone else might also be using.

Podcast interviews are about relationships. You're going to build relationships with not only the host but also the audience. I don't know about you, but I have never found myself in a relationship with any kind of app . . . sure, some might argue that these days we've created relationships with our scrolls of Instagram or TikTok, but those are one-sided and not "relationships." My goal is to show you how going a few extra steps in getting to know a podcast host before pitching to the host is going to both benefit your pitch and enhance your entire interview. As we get to Chapter 4 and discuss crafting your pitch, you're going to discover this in depth. Utilizing an app to create and build a relationship isn't how relationships are formed. The app might be able to gather information on the host, but it won't know how to relate it to you. Here's a quick example: I was researching a new podcast and headed to the host's website. I checked out her About page and saw that she had twins, her husband loved whiskey, and she'd left the corporate world. When I emailed the host, I mentioned all these similarities between us and how it felt like I was reading a bio about myself. Artificial intelligence isn't going to know these facts . . . because it's "artificial" in the first place!

If you're a podcast host and use AI for your show notes, that's something entirely different because you've already created the content with your podcast episode. Using AI as the basis for your pitch and topics and then as a means to send a thank you note is simply being lazy. As you read this book, you'll find that the most important aspects in podcast pitching and guesting is being authentic and genuine . . . being yourself and sharing your knowledge freely. The only way to do this is by investing your time in this process.

## USING *HOW TO GET ON PODCASTS*

I am so excited for you to dive into this book and get the most out of it, so I want to outline how it's going to work. There will be moments in which you need to grab your journal or notepad to write down your thoughts and answers to questions I'm going to ask you. I highly suggest you keep your notes handy when reading, because you never know when inspiration will spark. You might want to keep your notepad by your bed as well . . . or if you're like me, keep a note on your phone specifically for when inspiration strikes. Feel free to write in the book as well!

Every chapter will start with an introduction or overview of what we'll be diving into. It'll be high level and offer a preview of what's to come. You'll notice text boxes that relate the podcast pitching and guesting process to a dinner party. They're similar, because a podcast show is like someone's home and you're being invited into it as a guest. We'll head into the steps you need to take to accomplish the topic for the chapter. This will also be the section where you can find real-life examples that I'm sharing from my clients or myself. In every chapter there's also a sidebar explaining what the podcast host is up to. I want you to have a well-rounded and fully informed view of the podcast industry and landscape; therefore, I'm sharing with you exactly what a host and the host's team are working on—creating, producing, researching, and putting out into the world. As someone who has been on all sides of a podcast, I have this information I can offer you, so I am! You'll then be given an exercise that is simply like homework. These exercises will help you create your topics, put together a media kit, research podcasts, create marketing content, and much more. We'll wrap up each chapter with a summary of what you learned and how you'll use it.

## THE EVOLUTION OF THE DINNER PARTY

I already mentioned how I'm a fan of any kind of get-together, especially dinner parties. I get that dinner parties have been evolving so much that it's kind of rare to even use the term "dinner party." When you think of a dinner party, you might think of a black-tie, multiple-course type of meal. I have to be honest and tell you that I love that this was how dinner parties used to be. When I watch TCM movies and see that people would show up dressed to the hilt, I get a bit jealous. Who doesn't love dressing up and having a fancy evening? I know I do! These days though, "dinner parties" have been replaced with Netflix-and-chill nights and backyard barbecues with White Claws. No matter what our definition of "dinner party" is though, three elements remain the same . . . connection, conversation, and friendship. That's what these get-togethers are all about, no matter what title you give them.

Those constants in get-togethers are what make me compare dinner parties with podcast interviews. A great interview is going to create connections, include great conversation, and, the hope is, spark a new friendship along the way.

## WE ALL HAVE A WHY . . . HERE'S MINE

Over the past 5+ years, I've educated myself on all things podcasting. I took courses, read articles, and immersed myself into everything that goes into creating a podcast, marketing it, repurposing it, and more. I also took my 20-year corporate sales experience where my clientele had the highest of standards (they were celebrities, athletes, and some of the world's wealthiest individuals) and combined what I knew worked in the corporate aviation industry with the emerging industry of podcasting. I also had an awakening after I had my kids. I discovered that my purpose on this planet was to make it better than what it currently is. I had a duty to do that for my children and future generations. I found my voice and was no longer afraid to use it to speak my truth and fight for causes I believe in. I also knew that I had a lot of experience and knowledge that I could (and should) share with others. When I launched my podcast, I saw it all come to life. When I started to be interviewed on podcasts, I discovered just how much further my reach could be and how much of a greater impact I could have.

I don't believe in hoarding what you know. Many of us might have a secret sauce that we don't want to share, but the truth is that just because we share how we do something doesn't mean it can actually be mimicked exactly. You are your own person. You are unique. You do things your own way. I'm about to share with you my actual secret sauce, my framework, all my tips and tricks and tools. Am I afraid that I'll no longer have a business? Absolutely not. You are going to use the knowledge I'll share with you and apply it to yourself. I know that by helping as many people as I can, I will reach my goal of changing the world.

Every one of you now has the opportunity to share your knowledge, your story, your cause, your message with others who need to hear it. Take a moment and reflect on how massive that is. Podcast interviews have a ripple effect, and by writing this book, I've thrown the rock into the pond to grow the ripples. Now it's up to you to do the same.

Whether you're running for a political office, growing a nonprofit, sharing your experience or story with others, educating others on how to successfully do something, or being the light at the end of someone's tunnel, you're going to succeed by doing podcast interviews. Your reach is no longer relegated to just those who follow you on social media or find you on LinkedIn. You will now have the ability to reach people all around the world, and not only that, but your interview will be available for the eternity of time . . . at least while the internet is still around!

Podcasts are a life-changing medium. I recognized this the moment I listened to my very first podcast, and then I realized that I could help others change lives by getting them interviewed on podcasts. It's your turn to change lives with your message.

## EXERCISE

### Identify Your Goals

Yes, we have our first exercise, and we haven't even started on Chapter 1 yet!

Reflect for a moment on WHY you want to be interviewed on podcasts. What is your goal? This will come in handy as you read the book and during future exercises. Do you want to sell more books? Increase revenue? Land more speaking engagements? Are you a politician hoping to reach more constituents? What is your absolute hope and goal in being on podcasts?

Links, templates, and more content are located at https://michelleglogovac.com/htgop/ or by using the QR code.

# HOW TO GET ON
# PODCASTS

# STANDING OUT FROM THE CROWD

## USING YOUR KNOWLEDGE, STORY, AND EXPERTISE AS SPEAKING TOPICS

You've just tuned into your favorite podcast show and are intrigued because the guest is supposedly the expert on the same thing you are ... so you listen. You find yourself offering answers to the host's questions, and they far surpass the answers that the guest is offering up. Suddenly you're wondering why you're not the guest on this show because not only do you know this topic like the back of your hand, but you have so much more experience than the guest and could offer a ton more of tips and tools for the audience. Friend, not only have you identified what could be your first speaking topic, but you've also realized that it's high time you are a podcast guest!

So how did that guest end up as the expert for your favorite show? It might have been that the guest already knew the host, or it could have started with a pitch to the host suggesting this exact topic and it resonated with the host. All podcast hosts, myself included, want

1

to feature fresh ideas, unique voices, and interesting guests. We want to bring something new to our listeners, content that excites them, educates them, makes them want to share the episode, and ultimately results in increased downloads. We not only want this for our listeners, but selfishly want this for ourselves as well. We want our shows to stand out from others and garner attention, to have the kind of publicity that Joe Rogan gets simply for speaking his mind, regardless of whether we agree with him or not! So we look for guests who can help us do that, because any good podcast host (or business owner) knows that the host doesn't know it all. And just as a leader in business hires brilliant team members to help the business grow, podcast hosts look for guests who have something interesting to say to help their podcast grow. You are that guest who has valuable knowledge that a podcast will benefit from.

When it comes to what you have to say, you're going to want to know if someone else will find it interesting. It can be hard to define what makes you, your business, your expertise, or your mission unique. Every single one of us is good at something, but is it interesting enough to talk about on a podcast . . . over and over again? I know firsthand how hard it can be to promote yourself. There's often a mixture of having doubts and knowing that you just need to get out of your own way. This is where you must find your secret sauce—how to share what makes you interesting—and in this chapter, we are going to do just that.

The funny thing is that I've struggled with this personally, but I can define someone else's uniqueness and specialty quickly. I've had practice with the exercises in this chapter (and throughout this book) myself, and I've shared them with my clients, so I know that they can help you figure out what makes you, your story, and your expertise stand out from the others. In this chapter, you'll learn how to identify your areas of expertise where you stand out and create a list of specific and unique speaking topics that you can present to hosts.

Figuring out speaking topics is often the point in my onboarding process with clients that can feel like a therapy session. It's not at all unusual for clients to cry at the realizations they make, to bring up something they've never spoken about, or to reveal a part of themselves that they want to talk about but simply don't know how or if it would be of interest to others. When that happens, I know we're onto a compelling topic because the topic means a lot to them, and often it comes from a place of deep knowing or vulnerability. When people share this part of themselves, they can connect with an audience on a deeper level. It's truly the definition of being authentic, which is what the world needs more of. These moments point to the things that make them unique and why others will want to hear them speak on these topics.

Here are some of the questions I ask my clients before we craft their topics:

- What does the world think you do?
- What words describe you and your brand?
- What's your elevator pitch?
- Off the top of your head, what can you speak on?
- What topics can you speak on that are outside of your industry?
- If you gave a TED Talk, what would your topic be?

Your topic is going to play an important role in the podcast interview. It's going to be the overall arching theme throughout your conversation with the host, and the host's questions should focus around your topic as well. In Chapter 6, we'll go more in depth on how to prepare for interviews and questions that will come up.

## THE DINNER PARTY GUEST

Part of what I love about a great dinner party is the conversations that are to be had. My husband and I have a group of friends that we have monthly happy hours with, but if you want to know the truth, it's not really a happy hour. We eat a full dinner together and have drinks and dessert, and sometimes it even turns into an outdoor movie night. But I digress. The great part is that we have this time to catch up about once a month and discuss everything that is happening in our lives.

I don't know about your partner, but my husband will always ask me if I remember what shirt he wore the last time we all got together—so he doesn't wear the same one! Chances are that I will remember, but then our conversation will turn to what our last happy hour gathering was like and what was said. We'll chat a bit about who was going on what vacation, or if someone's parent was ill, or who had a job interview, and to remind each other to ask about those specific topics. We want to make sure we are present for our friends and check in on what had been going on in their lives last month and what has changed since then. We aren't all on social media together, so life events happen, and this is our time to celebrate those moments, to be there for each other whether we are sharing in joy or sadness or somewhere in between.

Getting ready for a podcast interview is similar to considering topics of conversation that you want to dive into with your friends when you next meet. A podcast interview will circle around a main topic, and you'll be thinking about that topic and what stories you want to share with the host as part of your preparation. Just as different social gatherings consist of different friends, podcasts will also have different topics or themes that you'll focus on, so each one will be different, just like your different groups of friends. As you prep for a dinner party, you aren't just thinking about what others have going on in their lives since the last time you gathered together, but what has happened in your life as well. If you're anything like me, then I know you'll have some stories saved up that are intriguing and good for a laugh or two.

# THE JOURNEY TO CREATING YOUR SPEAKING TOPICS

Before we dive into how you're going to create your topics, what they look like, and what categories they fall into, I want to introduce you to my client Elizabeth. Elizabeth came to me to pitch her to be interviewed on podcasts to help strengthen and grow her personal brand. You'll see the topics I created for her, and you'll see the results, and then we'll start work on YOUR topics!

# FROM BURNOUT TO CORPORATE WELLNESS AND CORPORATE BRANDING CONSULTANT

When I met Elizabeth, she'd recently left the corporate world and launched her own business. Elizabeth wanted to be interviewed on podcasts to help get the word out about her new freelancing career as a global marketing and communication consultant and why she left, but she wasn't sure if her story was one that people would want to hear. She knew she could speak on topics around her corporate background of marketing, advertising, and branding, which were fine, but they were all pretty generic overall. Elizabeth had an intriguing story about how the burnout of her corporate job landed her in the emergency room with a debilitating migraine. Hearing how someone triumphed over such an intense time in her life is empowering and moving, so I knew that part of Elizabeth's story had to be pitched because she's now working with C-level executives on incorporating their personal goals into their business goals. She wants people to understand that you don't have to go to the extreme of burnout to find your purpose and integrate it with your work.

Part of my initial process with clients is asking them to provide the speaking topics they have come up with. Elizabeth wrote, "I love to talk about our authentic selves ... what is needed in the corporate world to stay sane. I can talk about burnout, entrepreneurship, and my healing journey from migraines." This is a good start and allowed me to see where Elizabeth's initial thoughts were.

After spending decades in the marketing, advertising, and public relations arena, Elizabeth launched her own business helping C-suite leaders with their personal branding. She recognized the importance of a personal brand after her burnout in the corporate world because she wanted to leave her job at that point, yet hadn't created a brand for herself when she wanted to branch out on her own. A personal brand is how you promote yourself, but when you have a corporate career, your focus is usually on promoting the business you work for, not yourself. Creating and maintaining a personal brand when you have a corporate job is something unique and is catching on quickly, so Elizabeth knew that it was something she needed to promote.

Elizabeth's burnout story was ultimately about finding her purpose in life and recognizing that she could have a work purpose and a life purpose, but they didn't need to be the same thing. This was a topic I had yet to hear someone else cover. In addition to all of this, before she left the corporate world, Elizabeth asked her boss for help in managing her work to avoid future burnout; therefore, she had experience in how managers and leaders could better help their team members avoid burnout, as well as how they could all communicate with one another to ensure the mental health and well-being of an entire team was prioritized. Elizabeth was armed not only with a wealth of knowledge and expertise, but with topics that were unique to her.

After seeing what had been published about her online and talking to her, I created a set of topics for her. You can see her expert topics below. When we officially pitched to hosts, we included only the topic titles, but I listed the categories and my notes below so you can see what each of her topics entails.

- Life Purpose Versus Work Purpose *(signature method/ framework)*

    Elizabeth speaks on how you can have two purposes or passions in life. So often, we think we are only allowed to have one purpose in life; yet Elizabeth has discovered and is teaching others how you can have more than one and how to balance them both.

- Creating a Personal Brand Around Your Purpose *(skills)*

   Branding yourself is a new concept, and it's certainly not one that you hear in the corporate world. Elizabeth is helping clients create bios for themselves that align with their purpose and the corporate job they have or are striving to have.

- Living Your Authentic Self in the Corporate World *(business story)*

   All too often, we become married to our corporate job, and it becomes who we are. Elizabeth shares how you can stay true to yourself and your beliefs while still being in the corporate world with your career.

- Ways to Maintain Your Mental Health in the Corporate World *(timely and relevant)*

   Elizabeth has spent years ensuring her mental wellness is her priority, and she shares how others can do that for themselves through her experiences.

- How Leaders Can Navigate and Support Employee Well-Being *(experiences)*

   Elizabeth took a chance by telling her former manager that she needed to take a month off from work. She did so with advanced notice and explained why her well-being needed it. She talks about how business leaders can help create a safe place for open communication to support their employees . . . before they suffer from burnout.

- From Extreme Stress and Burnout to Business Owner: Elizabeth's Story *(personal story)*

   During the pandemic, a lot of people were experiencing burnout, but not everyone knew how to deal with it or talk about it. Elizabeth can bring it to the attention of more people so that they don't have to suffer from burnout and so that they can open communication and start to prioritize themselves.

The outcome? Elizabeth landed 15 interviews in three months!

## SPEAKING TOPIC CATEGORIES

Let's start with speaking topic categories to help you come up with the topics you want to pitch yourself on. A "topic" is your story, a way to do a certain task that you are an expert on, a learning lesson, a set of tools or tips that you can educate an audience on . . . all of these are categories that YOU can speak on easily because you're the expert. The topic is what you are letting others know you not only can speak on, but are the best of the best when it comes to it. You are the go-to person in your field. Your experience is like no one else's, and that's why you are the expert!

Creating titles for what you are an expert on can be one of the most difficult steps in this entire process. Do you start with your life story? Do you include every detail? How does your business come into play? How do you address the causes you are advocating for? Can you simply email the host a synopsis of yourself and what you do? This is where it helps to think like the podcast host. Podcast hosts are constantly thinking about what new content they want for their show, whether it's a topic they can speak on or a topic and a guest they need to find. By creating topic categories, you're going to be able to better organize your topics and also select specific ones that perfectly fit specific podcasts.

Say, for example, you have a marketing business. Your topic isn't simply going to be marketing tips and tools. First off, that doesn't explain much at all; it isn't specific enough. In fact, it's pretty generic, and generic is not what's going to make you stand out among all the others who could speak on marketing. Second, I'm sure a lot of people can offer tips and tools for marketing, so what is it that makes your tips and tools so darn special? Do you have a unique framework or method?

Give it a name! Are your tips and tools for specific types of businesses? Call them out!

I've created six categories for you to develop topics for. They encompass various areas of your life, business, and beliefs. Each category includes questions so you can start thinking about your own speaking topics. A best practice is to be armed with four to six speaking topics, not necessarily from each category. You might have two topics that fit one category and that will absolutely work. The goal is to get you thinking about different areas of your expertise that you can speak on, but might not have realized before.

## Your Business or Cause Story

The first thing I ask my guests on my podcast, *My Simplified Life*, is to share their journey to getting to where they are today. After interviewing hundreds of guests, I know that no one woke up one day knowing what career they wanted, simply did it, and retired from it. All the people I've spoken to have had at least one pivot somewhere in their journey. There are women like me, who discovered after having children that the career they were in simply wasn't what they wanted to do. Lots of people can relate to the yearning to do something more rewarding, to wake up every day doing something that makes them feel like they're giving back to the world, that makes them want to get out of bed and take on the day.

A corporation I once worked for had a great story about how the founders wrote their idea on a cocktail napkin with a pen one evening and it became a Fortune 100 company. Look at Sara Blakely and the story of how she started Spanx with just $5,000 and the red backpack she was carrying at the time of her first sale at Neiman Marcus. Anyone who knows Sara Blakely and her story has heard about the red backpack, and it's hanging on the wall at the corporate office as a reminder.

Your business didn't simply launch one day and become successful, nor did your belief in a specific cause randomly become a passion of yours. It has a story of its own, just as you do. Consider individuals—podcast listeners—who want to start their own business or are wondering if their current business will be successful. Your business story has the power to inspire those people and let them know that they can also be successful. My agency didn't start out one day with a big client roster and a ton of podcast interviews. When I started my business, I did event planning and social media management. I made pivots along the way that changed the direction of my business and fit what I wanted to do and the people I wanted to serve. Your business story is a perfect story to tell, whether it's a huge corporation, a one-person operation, or something in between.

Look at some of the largest nonprofit organizations and consider how they came to fruition. There's a story and a mission behind every single one of them. There's a story behind the people who launched the organization and those who work for it, because each and every one of them believes in the cause they are fighting for.

Your business story or impact journey will entail the steps you took to get to where you are today—the types of decisions you were faced with, the obstacles you had to overcome, and the pivots that took you in a completely different direction than you had anticipated. So often, we learn of success stories that seemingly happened overnight, but that's far from the truth. Years of doing hard work, enduring sleepless nights and stressful days, learning how to hire people, and much more go into launching a successful business. Sharing your business story is important because it helps others understand that the process they might be going through is absolutely normal, and they may discover that your business could help them in their own growth (resulting in more sales for you!). Oftentimes people aren't aware of certain services a business has to offer and how they could benefit from utilizing them, which is why learning about them through a podcast interview is a great marketing tool. I have had a number of clients tell me they had no idea that podcast pitching was something you could outsource to an agency like mine—turning your listeners into leads!

In Chapter 6, we'll dive into how to be a great storyteller, but now we're going to identify what story you have to tell. Answer the questions below, and give yourself time and space to write down what comes to mind. These will help you identify topics about your business story. You might already have the answers to the questions below, but I would encourage you to write down a few sentences at the very least in each area. This practice will allow your brain to start creating new ideas, trigger memories, and focus more clearly on your story.

- What led me to the job I'm in?
- Why do I believe so passionately in my cause?
- What gets me excited about what I do?
- What was my experience before that makes me want to do what I do now?
- What do I do in my job?
- How am I creating an impact to help further my cause?
- What is it about my job that I love?
- What makes me want to get out of bed every day and why?
- What's the best part of my job or business or cause?

## Timely and Relevant Topics

In the world of public relations, relevance and timeliness are everything! Podcasts are no different. As I am writing this, a big topic of conversation is all things related to gun reform, reproductive rights, and what it truly means to be a patriot. How do these things affect us? Will it change the way we do business, and if so, how do we adapt? I have clients who have a nonprofit that focuses on social justice reform and another who champions a variety of causes that include the rights of LGBTQ+ and women's rights. These are very timely topics.

"Timely" can be defined as something that is in the news or something that is currently going on with your business. Another great example is of a client who has recently certified her hundredth coach in her certification program and how the Great Resignation is leading to more people changing careers. This is newsworthy, timely, and relevant because it shows how the growth of her business is related to what's going on in the work-related zeitgeist.

Here are a few questions you can ask yourself to identify timely and relevant topics:

- What news topics are being talked about that are related to my business?
- What's trending on X?
- What articles have been published related to my industry, experience, and expertise? What valuable insight do I have into those topics?
- Is there a podcast episode I've recently heard that I could offer further education or value to?

## Your Skills

Whether you want to admit it or not, you've got incredible skills, and you need to talk about them. Your skills might include helping others negotiate the job and salary of their dreams, creating a website that stands out from others and is able to convey the exact message the owner wants, bringing teams together to work toward a common goal that otherwise seems impossible, teaching others how to perfect their storytelling ability, being able to sell without making it feel like a sales presentation with pressure, or having the ability to have uncomfortable conversations such as preparing for death and doing it in a way that is comforting. The list of skills that my clients have include some of these, and I'm sure you have some unique skills of your own. You are great at what you do, and people are going to want to know how you do what you do. This is part of educating and helping others. I sold jet fuel to corporate flight departments for 18 years. I didn't go to school to learn how to sell. I actually went to school to study law. For me to be in a career for 18 years selling one product must have meant I was good at it. I've taken what I learned and practiced in my sales career and applied it to my business and how I sell my service now. I believe it's all about relationships. I'm a skilled relationship creator, builder, and nurturer, so I can easily speak on this topic.

Let's take a moment to discuss if you need to "spin" your skills to make them sound compelling. To be honest, I don't think you need to do much manipulation at all. Let's take, for example, a client who's a book coach. A book coach is someone who keeps writers on track for their projects, offers input and direction on the writing, and determines whether it all makes sense. This specific book coach was originally an editor and has the skill of editing books, which is actually rare in a book coach because it goes above and beyond what a traditional book coach does for clients. Having the skill of an editor or book coach alone might not sound catchy, but think about the fact that she's a book coach WITH editing skills and is able to "kill two birds with one stone," as the saying goes. THAT is a skill that not everyone is going to come to the table with.

Here are a few questions you can ask yourself to identify topics about your skills:

- What am I good at?
- What skills do I have that I can share and teach others?
- What do people think I'm good at?
- What do I love helping people learn or do?
- What makes me the master of this?

## Signature Method or Framework

The way you do your work is unique, and I have found that oftentimes people have given a name to their signature method or the framework they use. It sounds complex, but trust me, the way you are operating right now is a method, and you just need to give it a title. Let's look at my framework a bit closer: The Podcast Matchmaking Framework™. I am "THE Podcast Matchmaker™"; therefore, my framework and title not only describe what I do but are unique to me and my process.

You might have a framework or method for what you do, but you don't yet have a title for it. I'm a big fan of talking things out, so whether you talk this out with a friend or with yourself, brainstorm on potential titles for your framework. It should be original, and it should describe what it is you do or accomplish with your work. Let Google be your friend and do some research. Go above and beyond and check out the patent and trademark office database. Check out your competitors, and see if they've used the same name. Take a few minutes to let your fingers do the researching, and you'll know pretty quickly if you have an original framework title!

Here are a few questions you can ask yourself to identify topics about your signature method or framework or to give it a name:

- Do I have a method or framework that I've created around my skills and business offerings?
- What do I call my signature method or framework?
- What's my specialty that I'm knowledgeable about and experienced in and would happily speak on?
- What do people think I do?
- What do people think I'm good at?

## Your Experiences

Your experiences are different from your skills because skills are things you know how to do, while experiences are things that have happened to you along the way. Also keep in mind that your "story" is the overall picture, while "experiences" are the moments that make up the story.

For example, one of the topics I cover is how I launched a successful business while my kids were still at home. When I say they were at home, I mean they were still in diapers and needing my attention all the time. At the time, I didn't realize how much work I was doing, because I simply did it. I was a full-time mom to two kids under the age of two who was cooking, cleaning, and running a business without an assistant. I do remember telling other mom friends that my plan was to start small, so that by the time my kids were in school, I'd have a business that I could scale to be something much bigger. I worked during their naps, got up at 5 a.m., took calls at the park, and simply did what I needed to not only build my business but also ensure I was present for my kids. It served me well and is a great topic because it resonates with moms of tiny humans and those who are about to become empty nesters.

Your experiences are also what helps make you relatable. People want to hear how you did what you did. They want to connect with you, and if you can show that you're just like them and were able to accomplish something, then it's going to resonate with listeners. Consider all the celebrities we follow and why we love hearing about their personal lives. We empathize with the Princess of Wales, Catherine, as we see Prince Louis acting like our own children, we cheered for Britney Spears as she regained control over her life and found love, we understand the fertility struggles of Gabrielle Union, Chrissy Teigen, and Savannah Guthrie . . . because these experiences make everyone human and relatable. I might not understand what fame is like for these people, but I can understand what they're going through emotionally because of my own experiences. Humanity is what draws other people in to want to hear your story. You become relatable.

Here are a few questions you can ask yourself to identify topics about your experiences:

- Why am I good at what I do?
- What obstacles have I been challenged with?
- What parts of my journey have been unique to me that I learned from?

## Your Personal Story

If you're open to talking about your personal journey and what has led you to where you are today, then by all means, it should be a topic! We all have a story. It's the journey of how we got to where we are at this exact point in our life. It's the decisions we've made, the experiences we've had, the moments in life that remind us what and who we truly love and what means the most to us.

Your personal story is another part of what makes you stand out from everyone else. For starters, it's your journey. Just like your business, you didn't get to where you are today by simply waking up and being yourself. Your path has had twists and turns, forks in the road, and you've gotten to this very moment because of the work you've put in, the decisions you've made, the experiences you've had, and the person you are. You have a different take on the world because of all of this.

Everyone loves to hear the story of others because it can be relatable. It allows you to get to know another person. All too often we forget all that we've been through to get to where we are. I know this is true for me, and I tend to ignore or pass over the twists and turns of my own life instead of recognizing and honoring them. I am who I am today because of the forty years I've lived, losing my father at the age of seven, growing up with alcoholism in my home, moving around the country in my twenties, miscarrying my first child . . . this is all part of my story and why I am the woman I am today.

Our stories can be a mix of good and bad experiences. There are stories of trauma in childhood and adulthood. There are stories of enlightenment. Everything that makes up who we are, where we've been, and where we are going is our story. Not all of us will be ready to share our entire story if it involves reliving the trauma that's been experienced. There might be outside reasons for not wanting to share it, such as a desire to protect others who were involved. If you're ready to share your story though, I encourage you to do it but to also be cautious. I'm a believer in therapy, and this might be something you want to bring up with your therapist if you have one before putting yourself out there. This is a very personal decision to make and one that you have to be absolutely sure of before you pitch yourself and your experience with trauma. My advice to you would be to know that by sharing this part of your story, you will be reliving what happened to you, and you need to be ready for that. You also now hold the power to help others who might be in a similar situation since they will hear where you are today after your sharing such an experience. Remember that your story is YOURS, and it's your decision if you want to share any or all of it.

*Trigger warning:* Here are some of the stories of people I've interviewed on my podcast: A woman witnessed her mother get shot in front of her but was never given the tools as a teen to process it and is now helping people understand their stress. A Black woman and a white woman witnessed two Black men being arrested for being Black at a Starbucks and are now leading a national movement to desegregate the public conversation about race and racism. There is the former federal prison inmate who witnessed multiple shootings as a child and, after spending over a decade behind bars himself, has become a leading criminal justice reform strategist working with celebrities and advocates as a voice of knowledge and experience. There's the woman who was leading the marketing efforts for Fortune 50 companies, but after a family member was diagnosed with cancer, she decided to move across the country to take care of her family and launch her own business helping small business owners. When you know and understand your story, you can then pull topics from it to use in your pitch.

Your story has also led you to perform your job in a unique way, which brings us to the creation of more of your topics. The way you do the work you do is unique to you. There are other agencies that do what I do, but none of them do it with the intimacy that I do. I don't simply create an email and copy and paste it to everyone who has a podcast. I work on creating a safe space for a therapy-like onboarding session so that I can truly understand who my clients are and what their experiences have been. I ask them to tell me about their entire journey. I also ask if their personal story or experiences are why they do what they do today. A great example of this is a preplanning funeral arrangement project.

I'm pitching three of the project leaders to be podcast guests, and they each have a personal story to share about deaths in their immediate families. As funeral professionals, one would assume that a death in the family would be an event that is smoothly planned out down to the last detail, but the truth is that the personal impact they experienced meant that their decisions were clouded by the feelings they were having. It's an important lesson that each of them shares on how preplanning is essential even if you are a seasoned funeral professional.

Here are a few questions you can ask yourself to identify topics about your personal story:

- What was my childhood like?
- How has it shaped who I am and what I do today?
- What lessons have I learned?
- What pivots did I make along the way?
- Am I where I thought I'd be?
- How have my experiences shaped what I do?

Let's look at the types of speaking topics and examples; then we'll dive into how to determine these topics for yourself. The list of topics below isn't an industry standard, nor do podcast hosts necessarily use this list. This is how I categorize expert speaking topics for the purposes of developing a list of topics to pitch. In the categories below, I include examples of my own expert topics:

- Your business story: "The Evolution of a Multi-Six Figure PR Agency: From Podcast Production to Podcast Pitching"
- Timely and relevant topics (such as something in the current zeitgeist or news): "Why and How Business Owners, C-Suite Executives, and Entrepreneurs Are Using Podcast Interviews to Grow Their Businesses and Personal Brands"
- Your signature method or framework: "The Podcast Matchmaking Framework™: Michelle's Signature Method for Landing Podcast Interviews"
- Your experiences: "How to Make Family Life and Entrepreneurship Work at the Same Time—It's Not Balance"
- Your skills: "Translating Your Corporate Sales Skills to Selling Yourself as an Entrepreneur"
- Your personal story: "From Celebrities and Corporate Aviation to Podcast Matchmaking: Michelle's Career Story"

Notice that my topics are pretty darn specific and that they highlight my knowledge and expertise. That's the level of specificity that's going to make your topic compelling and pitchworthy. Please don't go in with a generic topic entitled something like "My Entrepreneur Journey" or "Digital Marketing Today." These tell the reader absolutely nothing about your uniqueness. You want to create topics that are new and fresh, ideally ones that haven't been done before (or recently), so be creative. For example, look at my topic about why and how business owners, C-suite executives, and entrepreneurs are using podcast interviews to grow their businesses and personal brands. This is unique and specific because we know that these individuals can and are growing their businesses with podcast interviews, but I'm adding how interviews are helping their personal brands. It's specific, and I haven't seen this topic discussed anywhere else. Don't be generic with topics such as how to be an entrepreneur, or what are the best marketing tips, or how to use your voice or find your passion. These are all topics that you can find by using Google, and they're all things we've heard before. You want to stand out from the crowd!

## WHAT'S THE HOST UP TO?

When a host invites you into her home for dinner, she is preparing for your arrival. She has cleaned her home, created a menu, gone to the grocery store, prepped the dinner, and set the table. She has done all this especially for you. Not only has she spent her time preparing, but she's also spent money on the food and drinks she is going to serve you—all to simply enjoy your company for an evening.

Similarly, while you're busy crafting your speaking topics, podcasts hosts are busy as well. Podcast hosts set up their show much like the dinner party host has set up her home. They have created a welcoming environment and want to ensure you have a great experience and will end up sounding great when your interview is aired. The podcast hosts have taken their time and money to create their show and are offering their platform and audience to you, free of charge. Simply put, they're investing in you. We'll go over how to properly recognize the hosts and give them a big thank you in Chapter 6!

Here's a list of things that hosts have to do to simply launch their show prior to you ever listening to their first episode. It's good to keep in mind that a 30-minute episode will take about four hours to produce, and a lot of hosts do it on their own!

- Choose a microphone.
- Choose recording software.
- Do test recordings.
- Hire an editor (if not editing themselves).
- Select an interview software platform.
- Choose a hosting platform.
- Create cover art.
- Choose a title.
- Write a description.
- Select intro music.
- Create a project management board to track episodes.
- Outline the first three episodes and a trailer.
- Record the trailer and the three episodes.
- Upload all the recordings to the host software.
- Submit the RSS feed to other platforms such as Apple Podcasts, Spotify, Amazon, Google, etc.
- Write show notes for the episodes.
- Create graphic templates.

As you can see, it takes A LOT of work to start a podcast, which is why we won't be doing any copying and pasting on our end!

## EXERCISE

### Develop Your Expert Topics

In this exercise, you're going to craft your own expert topics. Start with a blank piece of paper or computer screen. Let this be your white space where you are going to write down everything that you know about.

If you haven't already, write down your answers to the questions posed in each speaking topic category above. If you feel stuck at any point, revisit your website and social media bios to recall what you tell the world and what you're known for. This is what you've already chosen to tell the world, so you want to make sure it aligns with what you actually do, and it should also pertain to the topics you pitch yourself on. (You'd be surprised at how many people forget what their website says!)

Venture out of your comfort zone and ask a friend or business buddy for thoughts around your topics and your story. Oftentimes talking it out helps. You can also review the topics that I created for Elizabeth and notice how I've strung together her experiences, expertise, and personal story to create unique topics for her to speak about.

Review your answers to the questions that you wrote down throughout this chapter. Try to put a sentence together for the individual topics as potential titles for interviews. Consider which ones sound exciting. Decide which ones are a "Hell yes!" versus ones that sound generic or plain Jane. These will be the topics that really light you up and you'll want to talk about over and over again. You want your topic titles to explain what you're talking about and grab listeners' attention. I want to also mention here that you might still be mulling over your topics, and that's totally OK. I'm a big fan of sleeping on it, talking it out, journaling about it, and allowing myself time to reflect on my topics. This is one of the most important parts of pitching, so allow your mind to wander a bit and come up with the right words before committing to a topic title.

I suggest coming up with at least six. Aim for variety in your topics, and focus on the ideas and topics about what you want to be known for.

It's good to showcase that although you're an expert in one specific field, you can speak to a variety of topics. By broadening your topics, you'll be able to pitch to a greater variety of podcasts, which we'll talk about a little later.

Creating a list of topics that you absolutely love might not happen overnight, so don't worry if you list some and then sleep on it and come back the next day with edits. Take your time with this part, so you have a list of topics that you'd look forward to speaking about.

## SUMMARY

Everything you have experienced up to this point in your life is material that you can and should use for your speaking topics. The trick is simply excavating and framing that material specifically for podcast interviews, which you learned all about in this chapter. If you completed the exercise, you have a list of speaking topics based on your business story or work experience, your skills and expertise, and perhaps your personal story that you would be thrilled to talk about. Next, you are going to include them on a beautiful one-pager—your media kit—which you will use when you pitch hosts!

# IT'S YOUR TIME
# TO SHINE

## CREATING A MEDIA KIT THAT STANDS OUT

N ow that you've identified your expert topics and the stories
you want to share, it's time to start working on your media
kit. I use the term "media kit," but others might refer to it as
a "press kit," a "one-page promotional kit," your "pitch sheet," or a "one
sheet." Regardless of the name, it's a one-page document that ideally
matches the look and feel of your brand. Its purpose is to offer everything a host needs to know about you that will ultimately make the host
eager to interview you. It includes not only your bio and website but
links to your social media platforms, your speaking topics, your headshot, your logo, and where you've already been featured. Your media kit
is a one-stop shop.

Before we dive deep into how to create your media kit, let's discuss
the fact that this is promotional material, and you might be thinking
that you don't want to promote yourself. This is a common theme I hear
from prospects and clients alike. I have the same answer for them as I

have for you. This isn't about you. Don't think about this as promoting yourself if you don't want to. Instead, focus on how you are going to educate others and share your knowledge and expertise with them so they can benefit from you. Don't get distracted by negative thoughts of self-promotion. Your interviews are going to help others, as well as help yourself and your business.

## THE PARTY GUEST

I recently created an Evite for my son's birthday party and wanted to ensure that no detail was overlooked. A birthday party or dinner party invitation should convey how your event is going to "feel" and how much effort you are putting into this party along with why it's special.

I'm all about the details, so when it came to my son's seventh birthday party, we went with a secret agent theme . . . to the point that I gave my husband and myself "agent" names as the hosts, the invitation was marked confidential, and guests had to "accept the mission" to RSVP. My goal was to ensure that parents knew the party would be filled with activities—seven missions to be exact—that it would involve food and fun, and that both of us parents would be present. There was an element of adventure, and it was so well received that the parents included themselves in the RSVP count along with their children—tripling my intended guest list!

An invitation to a dinner party—or in the scenario above, a birthday party—is similar to a media kit because it conveys your personality and sets up the look and feel you're going for with your party. Is it a fun cocktail party, or is it a black-tie event? What can your guests expect? Your media kit sets the expectations and the tone so the host has a sense of what you are bringing to the table—your personality, your professional "themes," and your experiences.

# LET'S GET ORGANIZED

Your first step is to get your house in order, or to get organized. I am a Type A person and love using sticky notes, organizing things, and having information at my fingertips. In this process, I want you to also love organizing your podcast pitches, tracking them, and knowing when they go live. If you have a favorite organizational tool, then you're going to want to start using it now to house all the outlets you've been interviewed on. You will use this when you research podcasts to pitch to and to track who you've reached out to and followed up with (which we'll cover in Chapter 4).

I've created a template included in this book and available for download for you to use for all your pitching purposes. But you can also make your own. If you love spreadsheets, then you can go that route or select a free online project management tool, such as Trello, Airtable, or Asana. I'm a big fan of Trello (www.trello.com), which is like a giant bulletin board with columns and room for all your virtual Post-it notes. Either way, you'll create the following columns:

1. The podcasts you want to pitch to
2. The podcasts you have pitched to
3. The podcasts you've sent your first follow-up to
4. The podcasts you've sent your second follow-up to
5. The yes response from the host but you're waiting on the calendar link, making it pending
6. When the date has been secured but the interview isn't live yet
7. Your podcast interviews that are live
8. Shows that ask you to follow up at a future date
9. Shows that you didn't get a response from or got the dreaded no from

My first suggestion as you embark on this organizational journey is to track down any interviews you've already done. I find that oftentimes we forget where we've been interviewed, so do yourself a favor and go google your name. You can add "podcast interview" or just "interview" in the search bar to help narrow it down. For every interview—whether it's print, audio, or video—create a row or card (depending on your data collection method) and include the link to the live interview. You're going to use this information in your media kit (as well as in Chapter 8 when we discuss your media/press page). Even if you're just getting started on your interview journey, chances are there is some sort of recording of you online, whether it was for an interview or a webinar or course you participated in. At this point it doesn't matter if it fits with your topics; we just want to be able to offer an example to hosts that shows you're capable of having and holding a conversation.

In the PR world, we refer to "press" as any outlet that mentions you or interviews you. Press includes websites, both digital media outlets and blogs where you have been quoted or have actually written the post, and print media, such as newspapers or magazines, radio interviews, podcast interviews, and television interviews.

For any press that you've done, find and copy the link for the interview or where your name is mentioned and also download the logo or graphic art for the outlet. For podcasts, you can google the name of the podcast and then go to "Images" and right-click to save the cover art. Keep all these in a folder, and give them recognizable file names so you can find them easily. You are going to use these graphics in your media kit. Logos and cover art are more recognizable than text titles and names. Images also tend to take up less real estate, and you need to present a lot of information on one page.

## DRESSING THE PART: ENSURING YOUR MEDIA KIT LOOKS AND FEELS LIKE YOU!

Your media kit should look like an extension of your website or the branding of your logo, whether that's for your business or personal brand. When someone looks at your media kit and then checks out your website, there should be no difference in look and feel. This is a part of your brand and who you are. This is what the term "brand recognition" means. It's like seeing the Nike swoosh without the word "Nike" attached to it, but automatically recognizing what the swoosh means. Brand recognition is seeing the golden arches and recognizing it as a McDonald's even as you're driving 70 miles per hour down the freeway. We want your media kit to have brand recognition and to offer the familiarity of your website, your logo, and your social media platforms. The look and feel are all the same no matter where someone sees your content. Consistency is a big deal in how your marketing materials are presented as well as in how you present and share yourself.

I always ask clients to provide me with their branding guidelines. Branding guidelines are an overview of what your brand looks and feels like. They include the fonts you use, your logo, and the hex or color codes of your logo, website, and anything else you create that represents your company or brand. If you worked with a designer to develop your logo and if you have a website, then these items should be readily available to you. Your designer might have supplied you with a mood board that has the color samples along with various names for the colors (a combination of letters and numbers), the fonts used, and possibly even some photos to showcase the aesthetic the designer was going for. If you don't have that, it's OK. You'll just match colors and fonts as best as you can when you design your media kit. Alternatively, this could be your opportunity to start creating your brand recognition from scratch.

## IT'S TIME FOR YOUR CLOSE-UP

One of my favorite movies is *Sunset Boulevard*, and my favorite line is when Norma Desmond says, "Mr. DeMille, I'm ready for my close-up." Not everyone is comfortable with a close-up, but it's necessary. You need a headshot. Why do you need a photo of yourself? Well, people want to connect with people. We are all virtual these days, so we want to connect more now than ever before. We have emails, Zoom calls, and social media, and so it can often feel like there's no true human connection. Having a headshot helps to create a human-to-human connection. A high-quality headshot is also going to elevate you as someone who is seen as a professional and who understands the podcasting landscape. Your podcast interviews won't always have a video component to them, so it's nice for hosts to see who exactly they are going to be talking to, and this is true even if there's a video component to your interview. This is part of being approachable and familiar.

Every host is going to ask for a headshot, so you might as well have one ready to go. Your headshot will be used for the graphics that hosts will make and share across their platforms (and you'll share these too, as you'll learn in Chapter 7), so you'll want a great headshot. I recommend investing in a professional photographer to take your headshot photo. Many photographers offer headshot packages, and some larger cities have studios specifically for headshots and social media photos. If you aren't comfortable with having your photo taken, you're going to need to get used to it. That's some tough love from yours truly! Trust me when I tell you that once you get that first headshot done, you'll feel much more comfortable about it.

Please do yourself (and me!) a favor and don't use the glamor shots you took in the nineties at the mall! Don't be afraid to wear bold colors minus any crazy patterns that can be distracting. Your background can be outdoors or a mono colored wall. If you've got a professional taking your headshots, then the person should be equipped and prepared with good lighting to ensure you look as natural and comfortable as possible. Some jewelry is fine, but be sure to not overdo it to the point that it takes away from you being the focus of the photo.

## TELL ME ABOUT YOURSELF

We now know what you look like, but we need to include who the heck you are, so you're going to need a biography of yourself. Don't worry; this isn't your autobiography in book form. This isn't even your life story in a nutshell. It's a two-paragraph description of who you are and what you do and should include some of your accomplishments and something that allows your personality to shine through.

Your biography should pertain to your experience, education, special accolades, and awards. If you have a company bio or author bio already written, you might be able to utilize that instead of reinventing the wheel. I think it's a good idea to have consistency wherever you can, including your bio.

If you don't have a bio already written, don't stress. Here are some tips for crafting your bio:

- Write it in the third person. This is what a host is going to read to introduce you, so as odd as it may be, write it like you're talking about someone other than yourself.
- The opening line should include your full name and what you do. For example, mine would say, "Michelle Glogovac is THE Podcast Matchmaker™, award-winning publicist, and host of the *My Simplified Life* podcast."
- Include two to three sentences about your experience—what you do, what you specialize in, and what type of clients you work with—and about your goal—what you are striving to achieve.
- Create a second paragraph that shares your educational background, the vicinity where you reside, and anything personal you might want to add. Mine includes that I have BA and MS degrees in law; I'm a wife, a mom of two just a year apart; a stepmom of two adults, and a fur mom; I reside in the Bay Area; and I have a love for wine.
- Don't be afraid to give your bio some personality and share who you are in it. The goal is to make your bio not only impressive but relatable as well.

Here are some good examples of bios:

"A natural leader in work and life, Shana Pereira has an empathic ability to bring people together and the intuition on how to make the impossible possible. With 20 years of experience in marketing and media, in her professional life Shana directs and guides large-scale operating systems that drive cultural engagement, fast growth, and lasting business impact. After a near-death experience during a heart and kidney transplant in 2020, Shana is now channeling her purpose into building a movement, content platform, and research institute around the future of religion and healthcare.

A storyteller, modern-day apostle, and unrelenting optimist, Shana is a sought-after speaker and thought leader sharing her insights and lessons around organ transplantation, the importance of partnership with your medical team, the mental resilience it takes to survive when faced with death, and the emotional impact of having seen the afterlife. Her experiences and speeches move everyone who hears them—guiding people on how to have a better relationship with crisis and, in turn, their own humanity."

"Sue Ruzenski, EdD, serves as the Helen Keller Services Acting Chief Executive Officer. Sue had previously been the Executive Director at Helen Keller National Center. During her 40-year tenure at HKNC she has led and worked with employees across the organization to implement innovative services to meet the identified priorities of the community. Sue has high enthusiasm for leadership development and mentoring, advocacy, and working in collaboration with partners to improve and expand service options for individuals who are blind, have low vision, or are deaf-blind. Sue is also the Oscar-nominated producer of *Feeling Through*.

She received her BA degree from Dowling College in Special Education, MA degree from New York University in Deaf Education, and doctorate from Teachers College, Columbia University, in Adult Learning and Leadership. Sue is an Oscar-nominated producer and the 2021 recipient of the LIBN Diversity Award."

"Nathan Phillips is Cofounder and Director of Concept Design at Technology, Humans And Taste (THAT). As co-founder of THAT, Nathan has led the development of a proprietary collaborative methodology, which invites diverse and unfamiliar collaborators to co-create innovative concepts for any medium, leveraging AI to supercharge any idea. What used to be art is now advertising.

Nathan has spent the last decade using everything he learned as an artist to collaborate with brands, nonprofits, and the occasional politician to make campaigns, concepts, and products that are designed to create desire in humans, drive engagement, and give people their own stories to tell.

He has worked in every medium creating interactive experiences for Broadway legends in Vegas, in breakthrough experiences like The Ride New York; he was a Blue Man for a hot second; he's shown interactive films at Sundance, IDFA, the Tribeca Film Festival; he's collaborated on digital art at MoMA, the Museum of Contemporary Art in LA, and the New Museum. Nathan has done performance art at the Whitney, won the World Press Photo Contest, an Emmy, and a big pile of Webbys. He also wrote a bestselling comedy book called *The Unorthodox Haggadah: A Dogma-Free Passover for Jews and Other Chosen People.*"

*A side note:* Be sure to update your bio—don't let it get stale. It's a good idea to revisit your bio a couple of times a year, although you'll be sending it out much more frequently when you are doing podcast interviews.

## YOUR SPEAKING TOPICS

Here is where you get to use all the work you did in Chapter 1 to discover your unique speaking topics. You are going to include those in your media kit as well, so be sure to have them handy and ready to go as you put your kit together.

## GETTING SOCIAL

We can't forget to include where people can stalk you . . . I mean find you! Gather your social media handles for where you show up most consistently. Since the actual hyperlinks are lengthy, I like to use the small icon graphics that represent each platform, such as the Facebook logo, Instagram logo, X logo, a microphone (if you host a podcast), and so forth. If you are going to use the Canva app (more on that later), then in the media kit template I've created for you you'll also find these icons ready for your use. If you aren't active on one of these platforms, don't include it. Each icon will have a hyperlink to your specific social media account, making it clickable and eliminating any need for the host googling you. If you're using Word or a PDF, you can also hyperlink your social media account handles within the document.

## MAKE THE HOST'S LIFE EASY: DON'T MAKE THE HOST GOOGLE YOU!

You might be wondering why we are putting so much work and effort into your media kit, and there's a good reason for it. One of the biggest points I want you to remember when you pitch to hosts is that you don't want to give them any homework. You don't want the hosts to have to google you, unless they really want to. Here's the thing . . . most podcast hosts have a full-time job or business and family that they are tending to. Some hosts might not even be in need of guests, but your pitch is going to knock their socks off and make them want to say, "Yes, I need to have this person on my show!" So if a host has a lot of other priorities, getting a pitch from a stranger that doesn't include any kind of link or provide any background information is going to be an automatic no. I know this is always the case for me. ALWAYS! This is why it's so important for you to gather all this information ahead of time, because you are going to house it in one gorgeous document for every host to see.

## PUTTING IT ALL TOGETHER

I want to make this as easy as possible for you to put together, so I've created a template you can use on Canva. If you're new to all of this, don't worry: Canva is a simple-to-use website where you can design basically anything. Even better is that it has a free option! The template I created for you includes a sample media kit and instructions on where everything should go. I recommend downloading a PDF file of your kit and naming it with your name followed by "media kit." One thing I want you to remember is that this is YOUR media kit. Let it represent you, your personality, and your brand and showcase how amazing you are. You can also use Word, Google Docs, or Adobe to create your media kit. This is about the end product and not about using the right software or needing to learn a new one. Figure 2.1 shows an example of a media kit, Figures 2.2 and 2.3 show examples of GOOD media kits, and Figures 2.4 and 2.5 show examples of BAD media kits.

**FIGURE 2.1**  Media kit example

**FIGURE 2.2**  Example of a GOOD media kit

**FIGURE 2.3**   Example of a GOOD media kit

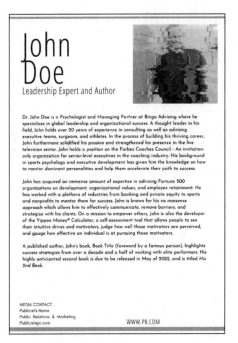

**FIGURE 2.4**   Example of a BAD media kit

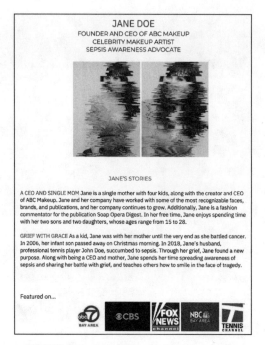

**FIGURE 2.5**   Example of a BAD media kit

In the examples shown in Figures 2.4 and 2.5, first look at how neither of these examples showcases the brand of the individuals. I assure you that their websites have more personality than what comes through in their media kits. There's also a lot lacking, such as their website addresses (URLs), social media information, speaking topics, and hyperlinks of any kind. Let's not be John or Jane Doe!

## CREATING A MEDIA KIT FOR A BOOK LAUNCH

Clients hire me to pitch them, but I also have clients who hire me to create a media kit and their speaking topics for them. One such client is Dr. Robyn Graham. Robyn was pivoting in her business and had just finished writing her first book, so it was time to prepare not only to launch her book but to market herself prior to her book being released.

Robyn set out to get new headshots taken and provided me with all the materials I needed. As with all my clients, we started with a one-hour call, and I crafted her expert speaking topics. I also read an advance copy of her book, *You, Me, and Anxiety,* to ensure I created and conveyed the topics she wanted to speak on for her book launch.

Since this media kit would be focused on her book launch, the speaking topics were related to her experience with anxiety and specific topics included in the book. Robyn's book brought about a new look and feel for her entire brand, so it was imperative that we included this in her media kit. We also included her biography, a synopsis of the book, and the book cover image on the media kit.

Not only did Robyn's media kit allow hosts to learn everything about her, but it also gave an overview of her book, and another plus was that the book cover image linked to the book's website. Robyn's media kit was "on brand," meaning the look and feel reflected her website and business, and she also included everything a host might be looking for, wonder about, or have questions about. Our goal was to make hosts say yes easily by giving them all they needed to know about who she is, what she knows, what her book is about, and where she's been. By utilizing her media kit, Robyn booked a number of podcasts that went live during her book launch week, which helped propel her to become an Amazon Best Seller and number one in multiple categories.

## WHAT'S THE HOST UP TO?

While you're busy creating your media kit, the podcast host is deciding on upcoming episode topics. Podcasts vary greatly as to whether they are solo shows, feature interviews, or are a mix of the two, and whether they have seasons, meaning they record a certain number of episodes just as a TV show does and then take a break, or they record every week or month of the year. Some hosts like to have a theme for a certain amount of time where they cover one topic in a variety of ways. Regardless of how the hosts set up their shows, they have to plan ahead.

On average, a 30-minute podcast episode takes four hours to produce, so many hosts, myself included, find it beneficial and efficient to plan at least a week ahead, if not more. I like to come up with topics I want to cover, and then either I will find a guest who speaks on each topic, or I will record a solo episode on the topic.

## EXERCISE

### Create Your Media Kit

You've done a terrific job gathering all the materials you need for your media kit, so let's create it! I love using the free website Canva, so you can go there and check out the template I created for you. You can also create your media kit using Microsoft Word, Google Docs, or any other system that allows you to save a document as a PDF. I suggest saving it as a PDF because then it can't be easily changed, and everything will line up and look aesthetically pleasing.

Here is the checklist of everything you'll need for your media kit:

- Font name(s)
- Color code/hex codes
- Headshot
- Biography
- Logo
- Social media handles/links and icon images
- Expert speaking topics
- Previous media and podcast features, including the links and podcast cover art and logos
- Your website URL

Now that you have all these pieces, you'll arrange them together on the page. It's a lot for one page, so you may have to trim your language and be judicious about what you include. Save it as a PDF, and it's ready to go out to hosts with your pitch.

## SUMMARY

Your media kit is going to come in very handy because it's a tool you will utilize in pitching yourself not only to podcasts but to any other type of media or speaking engagement. You've just created your one-stop shop that tells people who you are, what you do, and where they can find you!

# PODCAST MATCHMAKING

## FINDING THE PODCASTS THAT ARE RIGHT FOR YOU . . . AND THAT YOU ARE RIGHT FOR

A s a new mom, I remember taking my kids to the park to play. They would see other kids playing, go up to them, say hi, and ask if they wanted to play together. Making new friends was as simple as that. But at some point in our lives, making new friends suddenly becomes hard. We cling to made-up inhibitions of what people will think if we start talking to them or give them a compliment, and yet if we take that first step, magic can happen. New relationships are created, new memories have the potential of being made, and you might just find another person you can relate to, depend on, and be there for. The trick is finding people who resonate with you, who share common interests and might have similar goals and experiences as you do. Heck, this almost sounds like dating, but since it's been almost two decades since I was in that pond, I'll stick to the topic of making new friends for the sake of this book. The exact strategy you use to find new friends can be applied to researching podcasts to pitch yourself to.

Whether we are talking podcasts or human beings, it's not one-size-fits-all. Not everyone is meant to be your friend, and that's a simple fact, whether we'd like to believe it or not. Not every podcast is going to be the right fit for you, nor is your message going to be the right fit for every podcast. What is important is to find the podcasts that not only need to hear from you but want to hear from you. The ones that have your ideal listener or audience are the ones we want to reach. This all leads us to the questions of where do we find these ideal friends or podcasts, and are you sure there's a good fit for me?

I normally pitch my clients to 10 shows per month, and our contracts are 6 to 12 months in duration (sometimes multiple years). Every once in a while, I'll start working with a new client who asks if I'm confident that there will be the necessary 60 podcasts that I can pitch them to. Friends, I have a surprise for you—with over 7 billion people on earth, over 5 million podcasts (https://investors.spotify.com/about/) have come into existence; therefore, it's safe to say that there are definitely podcasts you're a great fit for, and there are people who want and need to listen to you. Does 5 million podcasts sound too good to be true? It certainly would be a HUGE opportunity for you, which it is. With COVID-19 in 2020, more people launched shows, and the number of shows did certainly grow to 5 million. Apple Podcasts has over 2 million (https://podnews.net/article/how-many-podcasts) on its own platform. And by the time you read this book, there will be over 3 million with an average of 2,000 shows launching per day (https://explodingtopics.com/blog/number-of-podcasts).

I'm sharing these podcast stats with you to assure you that there are more than enough shows for you to be interviewed on, pitch to, and share your story and message with. How many podcasts you pitch yourself to is entirely up to you, but please don't let the concern of there not being enough stand in your way. There are more than enough podcasts that will be applicable for your message, story, and expertise.

Right now, you're probably wondering how you're going to find these shows, and we'll get to that, but before we dive in, I want to share why it's so important to do your research and take your time during this process. This is literally the most time-consuming part of pitching yourself, because the ultimate goal is to ensure that you find the right podcasts; that they are current, do interviews, and aren't only solo episodes; that they have your ideal audience as listeners; and that they align with your goal. I get that I just threw a lot at you with everything you'll be looking at and for, but I'm going to walk you through it. We'll work on how to make sure every one of these steps is checked off before you even start to craft your pitch email.

## DINNER PARTY GUEST

You're ready to meet new people and new friends, so how do you go about finding the ones that you actually want to attend a dinner party with? You know exactly the type of friends I'm talking about! For me, I like like-minded humans who are organized, people I can depend on, people who secretly love reality TV and a glass of wine but are also masters of online shopping. They are outspoken when needed and stand up for what they believe in. Maybe this isn't YOUR dream friend, but it's a good description of mine! To find this friend, you might start to frequent places where you'll find people that interest you, such as a coffee shop or a local bookstore. I'm one who likes to be free with compliments, so when I see another mom at school pickup who has a great outfit on or an epic purse, I let her know. I'll introduce myself at kid sporting events or simply smile and make eye contact with other moms. It might seem too extrovert for some, but oftentimes this might actually lead to having a conversation and introducing ourselves. Maybe our kids are in the same class or we have relatives from the same tiny town in Nor Cal (it's happened!). Oftentimes it takes more than that initial conversation to decide whether you click or not, but as we all know, people show their true colors quite quickly, and you'll discover if that person is someone you would want to hang out more with. The trickiest part is putting yourself out there. It's scary stuff to be willing to face potential rejection, BUT as with everything in life, the reward is certainly worth taking the risk. It might also seem very extrovert of me to be like this, and that's true to some degree. Even if you're an introvert though, you'll need to start taking these risks in order to succeed with landing podcast interviews. The great part is that introverts love podcast interviews because they're one-to-one . . . no need to reflect on the fact that your conversation is going to reach hundreds or thousands of people—at least not right now!

When you pitch yourself to podcasts, there's risk involved. Risk that your email might go unanswered or that you're told you're not a good fit for the show. The first one will sting a bit, just as not making that personal connection with a new person does or not getting that second date. Learn from it, and remember that your audience is out there, just as your lifelong friends are. You will sit at that dinner party table and cheer with a glass of wine to cultivating new friendships and finding your people.

---

## WHO ARE THE PEOPLE YOU WANT TO TALK TO? AKA WHO IS YOUR IDEAL AUDIENCE?

Before we look for podcasts that are a good fit for your message, let's discuss who is your ideal audience. If you've spent any time researching how to start an online business, then you already know that defining your ideal audience is a big part of launching your business. It involves looking at the people you want to market to and what the best way of doing it is. Maybe you already have a client avatar and have named it, or you have an ideal reader for your novel. That's great practice for what you need to do next. Take some time to think about the people you want to hear your message. Who exactly is it for? This will intertwine with what your goal is for being interviewed on podcasts. Are you an author who wants to sell more books? Are you an activist or advocate looking to spread your message about a certain topic? Whose mind are you trying to change? Maybe you're a politician trying to reach voters or a business owner who is looking to reach more potential clients. Do you want to talk to location-specific listeners? Write down some of the words that are associated with your ideal audience, because we'll be using them when we go to research podcasts.

Some categories to brainstorm and make notes on are:

- **Gender.** Are you trying to reach a specific gendered audience?
- **Age.** Is there an age range that your message is geared toward?
- **Keywords for your topics.** What words come to mind when you think about what you do and what you speak on?
- **Geographic location.** Are you location-specific, or does your message apply to anyone, anywhere? Is it just for people in the United States, or could it be heard worldwide?

## HOW DO YOU KNOW IF A PODCAST IS THE RIGHT FIT FOR YOU? ARE CERTAIN ONES EVEN WORTH YOUR TIME?

As you look for podcasts that you want to pitch yourself to, you might wonder which ones are actually the right fit for you . . . or worth your time. As you're going to discover, a lot of research goes into finding that podcast. I not only like to have a well-rounded view of the numbers that are readily available about a podcast or host but also like to know who the audience is. I have had clients who present me with a wish list of podcasts they want to be interviewed on, and 9 times out of 10, they're really big ones. I accept the wish list and will use it as a guide for the types of shows they're drawn to, but I won't pitch to them all right out of the gate. This isn't to say that these aren't the right podcasts for them or that they're too big for a client, BUT the key is to know who the host's audience is and if it's the right fit.

Let's say your target audience is women 40 to 60 who are in the next phase of their career. They're looking for inspiration around having the ability to launch a second career or might be needing tips and tools on how to launch their website and social media. Now, let's say there's a show that has 1,000 ratings and the host has 500,000 followers, but the target audience is millennial women under 30. Landing an interview on the show might be good for clout, BUT you most likely won't get very much, if any, return on it when it comes to new business or book sales or whatever it is that you're trying to grow with your audience of 40- to 60-year-old women. This begs the question, why waste your time or the host's time on a pitch or an interview that isn't for the listening audience and won't benefit you (or the listeners) in any way? The answer is simple: There is no good reason why—don't do it. It's much better to focus on shows that align with your audience target, not necessarily audience size. A smaller podcast that has 20 ratings might actually have 1,000 listeners who all need and want to hear what you have to say. That's a much better potential than 500,000 listeners who have no interest or intention of purchasing your book or services.

It's good to look at numbers, but don't make that your absolute main focus. I'm going to share more about why numbers aren't the most important thing as you read on. I'm also diving into the importance of collecting additional information outside of just numbers and what exactly that kind of information is (and where to find it!).

## WHAT ARE WE RESEARCHING?

In Chapter 2, I introduced you to my Trello board, which you can use to track pitches and interviews and keep you organized with a repurposing checklist. In the template I've created for you, each podcast you pitch will have a card of its own. The information that you are researching and gathering will include:

- Podcast show name
- Number of Apple reviews
- Host's name
- Show description
- Show category
- Instagram account for the show/host and number of followers
- Contact email
- Relatable episode

The reason you are going to compile all this information during the research step is because you're going to use it to craft your pitch email. You'll also be referring to it when you're prepping for your interview and sharing your episode . . . more to come on that as you continue reading!

Some of this information will be readily and easily available to you, but discovering the right email address might take a bit more research and time. I've been doing this research for years, so you're going to learn my secrets and tips to make this as quick and easy as possible.

## WHAT PLATFORMS DO YOU NEED?

All you really need is the internet! You're not going to need any expensive subscription service, even though these services do exist. The online podcast show search engines tend not to have all the information you need at your fingertips. For example, there isn't a single platform that will automatically tell you if a show is solo or interview style. Some might offer information about whether the show is active in the last 30 days, but even if it does, you still need to check on the last episode to see if, in fact, that was the last-ever episode. Therefore, my motto is keep it simple . . . and cheap! Following is a list of the platforms that I utilize with a brief intro that says what you'll use them for, with a lot more to come.

- **Apple Podcasts** (if you don't have an iPhone, you can still use Google for this). Find shows with the keywords you've compiled earlier.
- **Spotify.** You can utilize its web player with its directory of over 5 million shows listed, also using your keywords to find shows.
- **Google.** Discover shows that might not be on the Apple platform, utilizing the keywords followed by the word "podcast."
- **Podchaser.** This website has a free option to search for podcasts, but you will need to create an account using your email address. It has various filters you can apply to your search to limit the country and language and find out when the last episode was released.
- **Instagram.** Hashtags are going to be your friend! You'll be searching for podcasts using the hashtag search option. *Spoiler alert:* You're going to find contact info here too!
- **Listen Notes.** You'll be able to discover how a podcast ranks among others in the world.

## SIZE DOESN'T ALWAYS MATTER

Before we embark on our journey of podcast research, let's talk a bit about how to define what show is worth your time and effort. I know a lot of people will look at how many reviews on Apple a show has and base its worthiness on that. Don't be that person. Doing so is wrong for a number of reasons. For starters, not all podcasts are on the Apple platform. Take, for example, Brené Brown, Joe Rogan, Michelle Obama, and Prince Harry and Meghan Markle—they all have exclusive deals with Spotify, which means that (a) their shows don't show up on Apple and (b) they don't have a rating or review system to showcase how big they are. If you were to base your searches and podcasts that you pitch to solely on the number of Apple reviews a show has, then you'd be highly amiss, as my example proves. Another thing to consider is that about half of American phone users have an iPhone versus an Android, which is why we need to ensure we include listeners outside of Apple. If you don't have an iPhone, you can't leave a review; therefore, over half of all podcast listeners are unable to leave an Apple review—once again diminishing the reason for basing your search preferences not only just on the Apple Podcasts platform but on their review system as well.

In the podcast research I've done over the years, I have also found that looking beyond Apple reviews and digging into the social media following of a host can give you a much more well-rounded picture of the listenership. I have seen shows with hundreds of reviews but only a hundred Instagram followers. Conversely, I've seen shows with a handful of reviews and 100,000 Instagram followers. This is when we see that either the people who make up the audience aren't engaged, or they're listening on other platforms. Another way to look at this is to see if the host with 100,000 Instagram followers has an engaged audience by looking at the number of likes for the host's posts. Does a post only get 10 likes? Then chances are the 100,000 followers might have been bought or simply have no interest in the account. I say all of this so that you have a complete picture of what an "engaged audience" truly looks like since we are talking numbers.

My advice to clients is to not focus on the number of reviews. Yes, it's nice to have one that has over 100 reviews on Apple Podcasts, BUT are the listeners ones who want to hear your story, who will join your movement, who will read your book or buy your services? The most important thing to look for is a podcast whose audience needs and wants to hear from you. This is why doing thorough research ahead of time is so necessary.

Another platform I love to use is Listen Notes. You can search podcasts for free, and it will show you a "listen" score that estimates the popularity of a show from 0 to 100 and a global ranking score that shows how popular the show is out of all the podcasts in the world. A show that ranks in the top 10 percent or better globally is considered great!

When you're looking at a host's social media following, be sure to not only focus on the number of followers the host has but also on the engagement the host receives. As I mentioned earlier, you can easily do this by clicking on one of the recent posts and seeing how many likes and comments were received. If someone has a following of 100,000, but the person's post only received 10 or 20 likes, then the audience isn't that engaged and the podcast might reflect the same thing.

## STARTING YOUR PODCAST RESEARCH JOURNEY—USING THE APPLE PODCAST APP

I call this a journey because if you're serious about landing podcast interviews, and I'm sure you are because you're reading this book, then you'll be researching podcasts continually for a while. With 2,000 shows launching every day (as of 2022), there are always new ones that will be applicable for you to pitch yourself to. I use a variety of platforms to research podcasts, and honestly, you can quickly go down a rabbit hole when looking for shows. Following that rabbit hole can be a good thing, as it will lead you to other podcasts, but it can also lead to a further time suck. Doing good research takes time, and the more time you spend looking for the right shows, the better your results will be.

So just how much time does researching podcasts take? On average, to find 10 relevant podcasts, you should allot a bare minimum of two hours for research. I recommend (and demand if you're on my team!) that you listen to an episode or two if you aren't already familiar with the podcast show. If you follow my recommendation, then add another three hours to that (or listen at twice the speed to reduce the time!). The reason for so many hours is because you're not simply finding the podcasts by searching for them; you're also gathering relevant information about each show that you will use for your pitch. Keep in mind that pitching yourself to be interviewed is NOT about YOU; it's about the host and the listening audience. This is why it's so important to have all the relevant information about the show and host beforehand.

I like to start my research on Apple Podcasts via the purple button on my iPhone. *Fun fact:* I didn't realize what that purple icon actually was for until 2018! Start by looking up shows that you've already listened to that resonate with you. Maybe you heard an interview and thought to yourself, "That guest didn't mention XYZ. Oh, I should have been interviewed on that topic!" If that's the case, you should look that show up and add it to your list of shows to pitch to. This is a launching point! You've already listed some keywords for your ideal audience, so you can use those to search for relevant shows as well.

What I love about Apple Podcasts is that if you look up a show and scroll to the bottom of that page, there's a section that says "You Might Also Like." This section lists shows that are similar to the one you are currently looking at and is a great way to start growing your list. This is also the beginning of your rabbit hole. I suggest you start by writing down these podcasts to begin your list and dig deeper into them once you've compiled 20 or so.

I am a fan of batching my work, meaning I like to do the same kind of tasks all at once. This is also why I suggest gathering some podcasts in general before diving too deeply into each of them separately. The first step is finding shows that you're already familiar with or ones that relate to them or include your keywords. Once you've created this list, your next steps will be to find the host's name, podcast show link, and number of reviews, all of which are readily available within the Apple Podcast app.

*A word of caution:* Before creating a card for each podcast in Trello, do a quick scroll through the episodes and ensure that the show takes guests. If the show hasn't interviewed anyone, cross the show off your list immediately. As well, be aware that although there are over 5 million podcasts listed just on Spotify, the truth is that not all these shows are active. The definition of an active show is that it has released a new episode in the last 30 days. If it hasn't, then it could be on a hiatus or break or have stopped producing new episodes altogether. Chances are that if any of these things have happened, the latest episode will most likely mention that fact! If the show is on a seasonal break, then make note of that to pitch in the future. If the show has ended, remove it from your list.

If the show remains on your list, make note of the host's name, the category of the show, and the link to the show (this can be on Apple Podcasts or elsewhere), and write down the title of the episode you listened to along with how it resonated with you. This will all come up in the exercise portion of this chapter, but I want to give you a heads-up that you should be looking for all of this as you go along.

## Quick Tip

If you are utilizing the Apple Podcast app and are also working with a laptop or desktop computer, you can copy the podcast link (three dots in a gray circle on the top right of the podcast) and paste it into your desktop browser. This will then allow you to simply copy and paste the rest of the information you need for your cards in Trello.

# SPOTIFY

You might think of Spotify as a music listening platform, but it's also a large platform for podcasts, listing more than 5 million as of January 2023. Spotify has an app, as well as a web player, so all you need is the web browser on your computer. Utilize the keywords you've made a list of and enter them one at a time into the search bar. Hit "Enter" and then select "Podcasts & Shows" to filter the results. The top row of results will be podcasts, and below that will be specific episodes that include your keyword. I recommend selecting "See All" under "Podcasts & Shows." From here you can see all the shows that have something to do with your keyword. If you click on a specific podcast, it'll list the most recent episode at the top, allowing you to see if the show is current. Spotify also lists the show description, and below that, it lists the categories the show is included in, such as business and marketing. This is a great platform for finding podcasts that might not be listed on Apple.

# GOOGLE IS YOUR FRIEND—EXPANDING YOUR PODCAST SEARCH

My stepkids grew up calling me "The Google Queen." Not only was "Google it" my answer to a lot of their answerable questions, but they knew I could always find an answer to anything via Google. My tiny humans now say "Can you just google it, please?" for answers they're looking for. It's one of my favorite tools on the planet, and it's also a tool I utilize when I research podcasts. You don't need a certain device to utilize the search engine, and you'd be amazed at what you might stumble upon.

When you search for podcasts via Google, most often the link for the podcast on the Apple platform will be the first to appear, which is great since we already know that gives you access to the link, host's name, number of reviews, category, description of the show, and all the past episodes. One of the reasons I suggest platforms other than Apple Podcasts is because not all podcasts are posted in the app. There are various reasons for this—perhaps the host has chosen not to, or the host doesn't want to obtain a username for the platform in order to link the show to the app, or the show might be a subscription listener-based one, or the show is exclusive to one platform, such as Spotify. By using Google, your results will include more shows and include the hosting website, such as Libsyn. This is important if a podcast host hasn't linked the hosting website to other podcast listening platforms.

Use the keywords you've come up with and add "podcast" to the search bar in order to find more relevant shows. Oftentimes the host's website will also appear. This will give you an opportunity to "stalk" the host a bit and learn more about what the host does. Be sure to write down any notes that might make for great conversation in your pitch email. I add this information in the "Relatable Episode" section of the Trello card.

*Fun fact:* I love to do extra homework on hosts before being interviewed by them. It's a great surprise when I can state a fact about them or ask a question about something they've done in order to show that

I care and haven't simply shown up for the interview for myself. We'll talk more about this when we get to Chapter 5 on interview prep!

## WHAT IS A HOSTING PLATFORM?

Every podcast needs to have a "host," and we aren't talking about the host of the show. An audio file is uploaded to a host, which issues an RSS feed. (RSS stands for Really Simple Syndication.) By publishing a podcast episode to one website (the host), it then sends out notifications of the new episode to other websites (i.e., Apple Podcasts, YouTube, Google, iHeart, Spotify, etc.). Having a host allows a podcast host to only publish to one website, rather than having to upload episodes to multiple places.

## PODCHASER

Podchaser is a podcast database. What I love about it is that it offers free and paid subscriptions, and I have found that creating a free account is very worthwhile. You can start by simply clicking on "Podcasts" at the top, and you'll instantly discover the top-ranking showings for that week. You can search shows by "Best," "New," and "Trending." Podchaser added a rating system in 2022, so this will be another area where you can see how a show is ranked.

Podchaser has filters so that you can view podcasts that have been "active" in the past 30 days, select the country they are in, select various categories, see podcasts that are similar to the one you are searching, and much more. If the host has claimed a podcast, you can also read the host's bio and discover where the host has also been featured.

# INSTAGRAM

Instagram is going to be one of your best friends throughout this process, so get ready to embrace this platform if you don't already. Most often, Instagram holds the key that is going to unlock the door to landing your interview—the email address. I'm always amazed that so many people don't realize that the contact information for Instagram accounts is right on their profile page. All you have to do is click on "email" or "contact info" to obtain it. It's really that simple. It might sound like magic, but it's information that is accessible by anyone with an account; and if the account holder has opted to put it out there, then it's OK to use that email address to reach out to the person.

This is one of the reasons I mentioned in Chapter 1 that you should have an Instagram account, whether you are consistently using it or not. It's a great tool to help you gather the information you need in order to be successful on your pitching journey. I use my phone and the Instagram app to access the account information for hosts because the desktop version doesn't allow you to view the contact information. Be ready to have your phone handy during this process because you'll be going back and forth between your phone and your computer.

You can search for podcasts via Instagram, which most people don't know. It's something I discovered, and people are always amazed when I tell them that I found their show via Instagram or that this is how I find shows in general. I search using hashtags and add "podcast" to my keywords. If you aren't familiar with the Instagram app, at the bottom you will see a magnifying glass. Click on that and type in the keyword you are using. For example, #businesspodcast. Click on the hashtag of the name that comes up, and then you can view the posts with that hashtag either by the ones most engaged or by the most recent posts. I recommend viewing the most recent because that will ensure the podcasts you are viewing are active.

Beware that at this point you could go down the scrolling rabbit hole, just as you did while you were searching in the Apple Podcasts platform. Check out some posts, click on the profile of the poster, and see if it mentions a podcast. You can then look up the podcast by simply googling it. You can also see if any of the podcast graphics that are posted have a guest in it or if there appear to only be solo episodes. I mention checking if the profile says anything about the account having a podcast because it could be that the person was a guest on another podcast, or it could be that the person used the hashtag to attract a certain audience . . . not helpful to us, but it happens.

From the Instagram user's profile (just click on the username), you will be brought to the person's home screen. There are clickable buttons below the person's profile description that are "Follow," "Message," "Email," or "Contact." Click on "Email" or "Contact" to find the email address. You'll want to document this on the card you created for this podcast on your Trello board! Whether you are using Instagram to search for shows or not, you will utilize the platform to find the email addresses that aren't readily listed on a host's website.

Why would a podcast host be on Instagram? The majority of podcast hosts are on Instagram because they are utilizing the platform to help promote their show. This is social media after all! When we get to repurposing your interviews, you'll be using Instagram as well.

## WHAT'S THE HOST UP TO?

The host is not only recording episodes continually but also creating additional content around the shows. Remember how you just found that podcast on Instagram? The host had to create a post for that platform specifically. Besides coming up with a topic, booking a guest, and recording and editing the episode, there are a plethora of other steps that a host and his or her team are working on. Social media content is one way to repurpose episodes so that more than those who already subscribe can discover the podcast!

## EXERCISE

### Finding the Right Podcasts to Pitch to

If you didn't already take time earlier to write down keywords, demographics, etc., I want you to do that now. To refresh, you should have a list that contains the following for your ideal listener/audience/podcast:

- Gender
- Age
- Keywords for your topics
- Geographic location

Start with a goal of finding five podcasts that fit your criteria. Utilize the various platforms (Apple Podcasts, Google, Spotify, Podchaser, Listen Notes, and Instagram) to find show titles and write a list down. Next, I want you to google each show to take a deep dive into the show and do the following:

- Find out if it takes guests. If it does, proceed to the next step. If it doesn't, cross the show out and move on to the next podcast.
- Create a card in Trello for the show with the show name as the title of the new card. I like to put in parentheses after the title, how many reviews the show has.
- Complete the following fields using the information from the Apple Podcast website you have discovered for the show via Google (or by copying and pasting it from your phone onto your desktop):
    - Add the host's name.
    - Paste the link to the show.
    - Copy and paste the show description.
    - Add the podcast category (this will be listed on the page as "business," or "marketing," or "society and

culture," etc.)—this is simply good information to know when you get a feel for the categories of shows you're interviewing on. Sometimes a show will pick a category simply because the show feels it will rank higher in it, making it a moot point in our research.

- Include the number of reviews on Apple.

At this point I continue to compile the information for all the podcasts on my list. You should be scrolling through the episodes, so if you have time, if a show has matched your criteria in that it (1) is current, (2) takes guests, (3) speaks to your ideal audience in the episodes and/or show description, and (4) hasn't covered your exact topic in the last few months, then go ahead and listen to one or two episodes that jump out at you. Jot down a few notes on the Trello card about it to help you be able to relate to in your pitch. For example, if a show features someone who made a huge career change, I would be able to point out that episode and tell the host it spoke to me because of my major career change from aviation to podcast publicist. This tells the host you've listened to the show and are not doing a copy and paste and praying that one of your pitches sticks.

Open up your Instagram app and look up the host's name. Sometimes the account will be under the podcast name rather than the host's name, so take your time to find the right person. I like to make note of the Instagram username so that when the interview goes live, I can easily tag the host. Make sure you make note of it to save yourself time down the road.

Look for the "Email" or "Contact" button to find the host's email address. Copy and paste it into your Trello card.

Continue this process until you have a solid list of 10 shows that you'll be able to pitch to.

# SUMMARY

You have just compiled your first list of podcasts that you'll be pitching to! This has been the major heavy-lifting part of the entire podcast pitching process. I know this step can take a while to get through, but I promise that you'll get quicker with all the steps as you keep going. Don't be afraid to figure out what works best for you, whether it's batching the research in a certain format or doing one at a time. This is YOUR journey, and this process belongs to you. Tweak it however you see fit. Just make sure you include all the necessary information in your research because you will be using it along the way.

# THERE IS NO
# COPY AND PASTE

## WRITING A PODCAST PITCH
## THAT GARNERS ATTENTION

You've laid all the groundwork, and now is the time where you get to put it all together. You will be using your beautifully branded media kit with your unique speaking topics and emailing the podcast hosts you've diligently researched. You're going to let them all know that you've done your homework and aren't just throwing spaghetti at the wall. You are serious and are ready to share what you know. You are a professional, and you are treating their show in a professional way that also relays that you are familiar with them and are genuine in your approach. Unfortunately, not everyone is like this . . .

Think for a moment about the direct messages (DMs) you randomly get on Instagram or LinkedIn. You know the ones I'm talking about—they say:

"Hey Amy, Love what you're doing! I have a marketing business and can help you 10x your sales revenue with what I'm doing. Let's connect! Best regards, Joe"

Um, Joe, do you really know what it is that I do, or did you just use the search function and a keyword or two to find my profile? As a podcast host, we get these too, and they can be pretty darn lame. Here's a recent DM that popped into my inbox:

"My name is Zachary, Former Marine Firefighter and author of the international bestseller XYZ Entrepreneur. I'm looking for radio and podcast hosts that would be willing to feature me on their show. My book will prepare entrepreneurs for the inevitable crucible—a turning point in their life—which will change their forward trajectory. I truly believe it will resonate with a lot of audiences. I would also like to know more about you, and what you do as well."

Notice how Zachary was obviously searching for "podcast host" and my name popped up, so he copied and pasted this message. It lacks any kind of personalization and reeks of laziness. For starters, he doesn't even use my name! *Hint:* My name is not only in my username but in my profile. How will your book prepare entrepreneurs? What is the "inevitable crucible" that you speak of? This "pitch," if we can call it that, offers absolutely no insight into what it is that Zachary wants to speak on, doesn't relay that we have similar target audiences, and tells me he just wants to get his book sold. If you want to know about me, check out my website, social media accounts, AND podcast! Make your pitch more about ME and less about YOU!

This is NOT how you will pitch yourself. Your pitch emails are going to highlight that you not only have done your homework on the host and the host's show, but also have quality knowledge you want to share with the show's audience and how the audience is going to benefit from hearing from you. Your pitch is going to be genuine and authentic in the truest sense without you ever needing to use the statement, "I'm authentic and genuine." Your authenticity will shine through in how you demonstrate to the host that you care, you've listened, and you want to help the audience as much as possible. You have done a lot of work up to this point, and it's going to come through in the pitch you send.

## WHAT IS A "PITCH"?

Before we jump into the pitch you're going to craft, let's discuss what a pitch actually is. I touched on it briefly in the introduction above, but now it's time to go into detail. A pitch is the email message you're sending to a host to "pitch" yourself. Traditionally speaking from a public relations perspective, this is an email you send to the media or journalists suggesting your story idea that you'd like them to cover. Within that email is not only a hook to grab their attention but reasons why the story needs to be covered, why it should be covered now, and why you should be the one they feature or interview about it . . . you're reeling them in. A tip that good publicists take to heart is to also tie in what the journalists have previously covered and to get personal. We are using these same techniques in podcast pitching, BUT there are differences, mainly around the length of the pitch, format of the pitch, and timing of follow-ups. I'm going to educate you on those nuances that will put your pitch at the top and get that yes! You're also going to get a leg up on many publicists who don't know these subtle differences, making your pitch rise even further to the top!

In podcasting, your pitch is being sent to the host (or sometimes the producer), and it highlights your expertise and the value you will bring to the show. You are going to relate to the host and get personal. You're also going to discover the art of the follow-up and not only how to properly follow up but when to follow up as well.

# SENDING THE EMAIL

I have had some pretty epic guests on my podcast . . . at least I fangirl over a lot of them! I can't tell you the number of times I've been asked HOW I have landed some of my guests, and my answer is always simply that I emailed them and asked. I realize that is incredibly basic, but it's true. The difference in my email versus others they might receive though is that it's extremely personal. I practice what I preach when it comes to asking guests to come on my podcast—I do it in the exact same manner that I use when I pitch my clients to podcasts and media outlets. How does one get personal with a stranger? You don't even have to "stalk" them, as I like to call it. Spend some time reading what they've put out into the world for others to learn about them.

A great example of this is Zibby Owens. This woman has created a book media empire in a short amount of time and is growing leaps and bounds on a daily basis. I was intrigued and wanted a chance to get to know who she was and maybe, just maybe, have a conversation with her. My first step was buying her book, *Bookends*, and reading it cover to cover. Want to know what's on the last page of her book? Her personal email address where she basically says if you've gotten this far, send me a note and let me know what you think. You literally don't have to tell me twice—I emailed her the night I finished the book, and want to know what happened? She emailed me back!

I shared specific parts of her book that really stuck with me, the life moments I found we had in common and people we both knew, and ultimately I asked if she would be a guest on my show. She graciously accepted, and we had the best conversation both on and off the air. I know this happened not only because I put myself out there, but because I was willing to learn what I could about Zibby beforehand and was greeted with the gift of her email address for doing so. Take the time and steps to learn about the person you're pitching to, and your efforts will be rewarded.

# CRAFTING YOUR PITCH BLUEPRINT TEMPLATE—THERE IS NO COPY AND PASTE

There is no copy and paste in PR. That's my number one rule and a rule that all publicists SHOULD abide by; yet there are a number that don't. This is a big part of what sets publicists apart from each other and what is going to set you apart from the majority of pitches that hosts receive. There will be a very small portion of your pitch email that will remain the same in all your emails, and I call this your skeleton pitch because you build on it. This includes the titles of your topics. Those aren't going to change with every pitch, but which topics you pitch will change for each podcast.

In addition to originality and personalization, the major point of your pitch email is to ensure the host doesn't have to do any kind of homework or research outside of your email. This means everything needed to say yes is included in your email. Do you want to know what kind of pitch gets an automatic NO from me? When there's not a single link included in the pitch. It's as simple as that. Add a hyperlink to your name that sends me to your website; hyperlink a recent podcast interview; attach your media kit . . . make your pitch email a one-stop shop!

I've said it before, and it's worth saying again: A host usually has a full-time job outside of doing a podcast. Time is limited, and as the saying goes, time is money. If a pitch hits an inbox without all the information it takes to say yes, then it's going to be a no. If the host needs to leave your email in order to find out who you are by launching a Google search or opening Instagram to look up that you exist (outside of just clicking on the link you provided), then you've completely missed the mark on your pitch email. You've just created more work and taken time away from the host. In essence, even if your pitch truly relays that you have done your homework on the host, yet you haven't made it easy for the host to know who you are, your pitch will seem that it is actually all about you because you couldn't be bothered to provide all the information necessary in your email. Not to worry though, because I'm going to make sure that your pitch includes everything it needs!

Your pitch emails will consist of the same type of content, an outline per se, so I've created a basic podcast pitch blueprint. Your podcast pitch blueprint is outlined below, and you'll follow this format with every pitch you send. After you review the format, I've got examples for you as well!

1. Subject line with your name included
2. Friendly opening using the host's name (spelling counts!)
3. Episode you enjoyed and how you related to it, as well as to anything personal to the host
4. Two sentences about you with your name hyperlinked to your website
5. Two to three topics from your media kit that you feel are the best fit for the show you are pitching to
6. A few places you've recently been interviewed that are hyperlinked to the actual interviews
7. Friendly closing that says your media kit is also attached
8. Your name

The parts that will remain the same in every pitch are parts 4 and 6: the two sentences about you and the places you've recently been interviewed. Of course, the interviews will get updated as you land more recent interviews, but overall, everything else in the email will be unique to the host you are reaching out to.

When it comes to the subject line, I always like to use the name of the podcast and the name of the guest being pitched. For example, a pitch to my show would be *"My Simplified Life* Podcast Guest— Michelle Glogovac." This helps me immediately recognize the show I'm pitching and keeps things organized when a reply comes in. It also makes the email more easily searchable in your sent folder for when it's time to follow up. You're also starting out by acknowledging the name of the podcast to the host and stating that your email is in regard to a podcast guest and the person's (your) name. This helps the host keep track of her or his own guest requests as well. If there's something that makes it easier for me to search my inbox or glance at an email and match a subject line with exactly what I'm looking for, then I'm all for it.

ALWAYS use the host's name(s) in your greeting. The podcast world is pretty casual, so there's no need to address the host as Ms. or Mr., especially if you aren't sure what title or pronouns the host goes by. The names of the hosts are listed with their podcast listing/description on Apple Podcasts, Spotify, or anywhere else you're looking, so greet them by their first name. And for the love of all things, please make sure you spell it correctly! I go against using "Dear" in your greeting because I feel it's really formal and not really email language, but that's my personal opinion. If "Hi" is too informal for you, use "Good morning" or "Good afternoon" along with the host's name. Please, please, please spell the person's name correctly (yes, I'm repeating myself!). I've seen journalists and hosts complain about their name being incorrect or someone using their IG or X handle as their name. Don't be that person! This is another reason why I notate the host's name on the Trello card when doing research! Getting someone's name wrong sets the tone negatively for the rest of your email, and we certainly want to start off on the right foot.

Next, you're going to dive into what you like about the show and mention the episode(s) you listened to. This is really your time to highlight that you've listened to the show and are genuinely interested in the content the host is putting out for the listeners. At this point, you should also start to share yourself with the host. If an episode resonated with you because of an experience you had, share that. This is what the true definition of being authentic actually means. I've shared how my father passed away when I was seven with a host because the particular episode I listened to addressed this topic. I've also shared how I started my business with two tiny humans at home and the struggles I had as well as the excitement along the way. This also seems to be the hardest part of the pitch for many. I say that because it's the most frequently left-out part of the email. For some reason, many think it's enough to just share themselves and not relate to the person on the receiving end of the email. THIS section is going to set you miles apart from other pitches!!!!

One of the biggest reasons this is left out of a pitch is because this part takes time. You've spent time looking up shows that are a good fit. You've spent time gathering the contact information. But now I'm telling you that you also need to take time to actually listen to an episode or two and connect with it? YES! Listening to an actual episode gives the host another download, and it shows the host that you truly do know what the show is about. Take it one step further and leave a review and rating! These small acts of kindness really help a podcaster out and show that you're not in this just for yourself.

Next, be sure to weave in a sentence about why your knowledge, expertise, or message is one that the audience will benefit from hearing. Why is it important for the audience to hear about this specific topic from you? The key to remember is that this section is NOT about YOU! Wait, Michelle, didn't you JUST say that I need to include why the audience needs to hear my topic? I know this sounds like it's completely contradictory to what you're actually writing, but your email is about the host and the audience! The ONLY exception to this section is if you know the host personally and have a longstanding relationship. Then, and ONLY then, can you be more casual about your pitch email. When I work with a host more than once or twice, the host knows I'm a listener of the show. We have already established a relationship; therefore, I will omit the recent episode part and simply let the host know that I have a new client that I think would be a great fit for the show and move on to the next steps. DO NOT SKIP this step otherwise!

When I say that this is about the host and the audience and not about you, I'm emphasizing that you need to provide reasons why exactly the audience is going to benefit from hearing an interview with you. Don't mention that you want to sell or promote your book or gain more voters or sell your services. *NO!* (Yes, I'm yelling!) What has made you the expert on this, and what makes you stand out that the audience has to hear it from YOU and no one else? This is where you need to take time to distinguish yourself from those like you or anyone who does something similar to what you do. For example, I'm a publicist, but specializing in podcasts is a big differentiator from other publicists. There are not many publicists like me, especially not ones who work with other publicists and PR agencies pitching their clients to podcasts. I'm different, and that's what I present to a host. I came from the corporate world and launched a new career in a new industry . . . another unique part about me. I started a multi-six-figure business with two kids at home. What sets you apart?

Now that you've let the hosts know that you listen to their show and want to help their listeners, share a couple of sentences about yourself. Who are you? What are you known for? What do you do? Be sure to hyperlink your name or title or company or book to your website. *Sidenote:* Hyperlinking is when you select certain text and link it to a website. This can be considered a mini, mini bio of yourself. It's succinct and doesn't give the full 411 on where you've been educated, awards you've won, jobs you've held, and so on. Make this short and sweet, but also informational. After saying who you are, let the host know that some of your expert speaking topics include the following and bullet-point two or three of your topics that are the best fit for the show. You'll be attaching your media kit, so hosts will always have the opportunity to decide on an alternative topic if they see one they prefer or think is a better fit.

Hosts love to be able to see and hear other shows you've been interviewed on. By highlighting a couple of previous interviews, you allow them to see that you are capable of being interviewed and can and will professionally show up and speak, while also laying the foundation that you're already in demand. If you haven't been interviewed on a podcast before, feel free to include any interview or video of you, even if the topic isn't related to the ones you are proposing. The purpose of this is to show that you can be interviewed and speak intelligently. It's simply an example of your capabilities. This is also a perfect opportunity both to show how well you can speak and to show that you're set up to do an interview. You have the necessary equipment (mic and headset) and know what good sound quality means!

Wrap up your email by saying that you've attached your media kit with additional speaking topics and welcome any questions the hosts might have. Thank them, and sign off with your name. And don't forget to attach your media kit!

## SAMPLE SKELETON PITCH EMAIL

Here's an example of a pitch that one of my team members sent out on behalf of one of our clients. Every single one of The MLG Collective team members uses this skeleton pitch to craft their unique emails to hosts. It's proved to be successful thousands of times over, not only in landing interviews but in receiving rave reviews from hosts on how personalized it is!

---

**Subject:** Podcast Guest—Merle R. Saferstein

**Friendly opening:** Hi Bianca, Carly, and CeCe,

**Episode:** I enjoyed listening to your podcast episode with Roz about his writing school. I think this is such a good idea for children. As a previous classroom teacher, I know the importance of helping our children learn to express themselves and supporting them. I wanted to reach out to you to introduce one of my clients, Merle R. Saferstein, as a potential podcast guest because she shares her story about journaling and her writing process for her journals and book.

**About:** Merle R. Saferstein is an educator, speaker, and author. She has been journaling for 48 years and has amassed a collection of 380 journals, the majority of which are the basis for her legacy journal *Living and Leaving My Legacy, Vol. 1. Living and Leaving My Legacy* has already received

---

praise from Meta's COO Sheryl Sandberg and Lynda Monk, Director of The International Association for Journal Writing, and is set to launch June 7, 2022.

**Highlighted topics and why:** Merle's experience as a Holocaust educator for 26 years, wife of 55 years, and mother of two and her dedication to journaling makes her not only incredibly unique, but someone who is filled with stories, life lessons, and is the definition of a woman who was years ahead of her time. Some of her expert topics include:

- Journaling—Finding Value in Writing
- Legacy Journaling—How You Live Your Life Will Become Your Legacy
- The Book Writing Process

**Recent interviews:** Merle has been featured in <u>Authority Magazine</u>, <u>Thrive Global</u>, <u>HuffPost</u>, and <u>The Make Meaning</u> podcast and in a number of other outlets. I've also attached her media kit for your review with more of her featured speaking topics and bio.

Please let me know if you have any questions at all.

**Friendly closing:** Thank you!
**Your name:** Tiffany

Notice that every section of the blueprint is addressed within the pitch email and hyperlinks (notated as underlined) are included throughout. This provides all the information the host needs in one email. Once you've sent the email, be sure to make a note on your Trello card stating that you've emailed the host and the date you sent the email; then move the card from "Potentials to Pitch" to the "Initial Email" column.

Another tip I have when using Trello is to create color-coded labels for the month that I'm sending a pitch. I use a rainbow-ordered system (red, orange, yellow, green, blue, purple, pink, and so on) to help keep track easily of the order in which I send a pitch. This allows you to not have to go into each card for every podcast to see when you sent the first email.

## THE ART OF THE FOLLOW-UP

I worked in sales for almost two decades and will never forget the statistic that says that on average it takes seven touches to make a sale. In most cases, I closed the sale in fewer touches, but that stat was my motivating factor to not get discouraged if I didn't land a new client on the first try. I always started with an email, then followed up with a phone call to see if I could drop by with some cookies (because who doesn't love that?!), an in-person visit, and a handwritten thank you card; and by then, not only had I created a relationship with the prospective client, but I had made a sale. In all these interactions, I was never aggressive or annoying. Yes, I was persistent, but in a gentle, nonthreatening way. This is the art of the follow-up.

When you think of sales, you think of buying a car. No one likes a used car salesman. Used car salesmen have a reputation of being pushy and that they only want the sale and will hound you until you get so utterly annoyed that you either leave the lot without a car or purchase a car and feel foolish about it. It should be the goal of every salesperson, publicist, and you, since you're pitching yourself, to never come off as a used car salesman. Sales doesn't have to be sleazy, annoying, or gross. To me, sales is about a relationship, and when you truly care about the person you're selling to and the product/service you're selling, that will shine through.

I compare the job of pitching clients with my previous sales career because the two have a lot in common. You have to believe in the product or service you're selling. As a publicist, I have to believe in the clients I'm promoting. If you don't believe in what you're selling or saying, the person you're speaking to is going to feel that vibe. The inauthenticity is sure to shine through, just as it will when you don't genuinely care about what you're selling. When I craft a pitch for a client that I am excited about, it more than comes through. I will get so pumped up about what a client has to say, and it will motivate me to pitch the client in a way that is unlike any other . . . because I know the client's story, I believe in it, and I want the world to hear it. I know it's going to change lives, and it becomes my mission to get my client out there.

My personal technique for cold calls focuses on the importance of creating relationships with prospective clients. The same can be said when I am emailing a podcast host in the hope of creating a mutually beneficial relationship. You need to convey that you really are not just wanting to be on the show but have a genuine interest in reaching the listeners with what you know will be beneficial to them. This isn't just about you. This isn't about getting you in the spotlight and pumping you up to the host. Always, always remember that this is about helping others, educating others, letting them learn from you. If you truly believe that people need to hear what you have to say because it's going to benefit them, it will be obvious in your pitch.

Your follow-up should be light and friendly, just as your pitch was. There's no need to reply by saying you're bumping your message up to the top of the host's inbox or that you want to make sure your email was seen. I'm more than positive that the reason your initial pitch wasn't replied to was because either the host was distracted and forgot to respond, or the host thought it simply wasn't a good fit. Your follow-up should be concise—short and sweet but also professional. In the following pages, you'll see some examples of really bad follow-up emails that I've actually received along with what your follow-ups should look like. I'm hoping that you'll be able to spot the bad parts right away, but I'll also point them out to ensure you don't make these same mistakes.

## Follow-Up Timing

You've sent your initial pitch and now you wait. But how long do you wait? Since I'm someone who tends to be very impatient, waiting for my inbox to ding is something I'm not good at. In the media world with breaking news changing by the minute, follow-ups are sent within 24 hours, BUT podcasting is the total opposite. Podcast interviews are not breaking news, for the most part. They don't need to be booked and scheduled within the week. So if you're impatient, then welcome to your new journey of practicing patience. I recommend following up on your initial email two to three weeks after sending it. Send a second follow-up two to three weeks after that. One of the first reasons for the follow-up is to ensure that your email didn't go into the recipient's spam folder. Trust me when I say this has happened to me more than once.

When sending your follow-up, go to your sent folder and reply to the initial email you originally sent. This will ensure that the host knows what you're referencing and all the information from the first pitch email will already be included. You can do this again when you send your second follow-up email.

The artful part of a follow-up is in your wording. Concise and to the point are the keys to a good follow-up. Please don't get discouraged if you don't receive a response right away. Although I have had great luck with booking a client on the first email, that's often not the case. But more often than not, I receive replies from my follow-ups, which is what makes them so important. Hosts get busy and appreciate a kind follow-up, so don't worry if you haven't received a yes or no response. In fact, as I'm writing this book, I received an email from a host wanting to interview one of my clients this month . . . 10 months after I sent the initial pitch and follow-ups! Yes, this is rare because 10 months is a long time, but since podcast pitching is a form of PR and PR is a long game, think of this as a marathon and not a sprint! You're in this for the long run and should welcome interviews whether they happen this week, next month, or even 10 months from now.

## Example of a First Follow-Up Email

Hi [*name*],

I'm following up on my email in regard to potentially being a guest on your show. I'd love to further discuss such an opportunity with you.

Thanks so much!
Michelle

This email is short and to the point. It's perfect because it doesn't take much time and can refresh someone's memory about your original email. For my follow-ups, I go to my sent folder, search for the email by podcast name and simply hit "reply" to the initial email I sent to the host. This way your follow-up includes all the original pitch and links you already sent!

## Example of a Second Follow-Up Email

Hi [*name*],

I'm checking in one last time to see if you might be interested in having me share my knowledge on *<subject>* with your audience.

Thank you!
Michelle

My favorite part of this example is that you are letting the host know that there is no need to worry about hearing from you again, but it also relays the urgency that you won't be sending another reminder about having you on the show. It's incredible how many replies I will receive to a final follow-up email, and most times it's to thank me for not giving up on the silence and that the host simply forgot to reply.

With both follow-ups, be sure to mark your activity on your Trello card and move the card to the "Follow Up" column. After the second follow-up, if I haven't heard anything, I assume it's a no and move it to the "No Thank You" column. Don't worry—you can always move the card to "Pending" when the host comes back with a yes!

# DOS AND DON'TS OF PITCHING

In a nutshell, here are the dos and don'ts of pitching:

**DO**

- Get personal in your pitch.
- Share what you love about the podcast.
- Include links to your website and recent interviews.
- Suggest two or three speaking topics that best resonate with the show.
- Attach your media kit.
- Follow up two to three weeks after your initial pitch.
- Follow up once more, two to three weeks after your first follow-up.

**DON'T**

- Copy and paste.
- Send an email without any links.
- Give the host homework by needing to google you.
- Follow up within the first week of your pitch.
- Be annoying or aggressive in your wording.
- Make it all about you.

# EXAMPLES OF BAD PODCAST PITCH EMAILS

These are REAL email pitches I've received in my inbox. I've copied and pasted them as examples. Only the names of people, companies, and the book that one of them wrote have been changed to protect the identity of the senders of these really bad pitches.

## Example #1

> Hey, how's it going! Are you currently looking for guests for your podcast? We work at ABC Law Group with CEO John Doe that would love to be a guest on your podcast. The main topics we can talk about are Law and Marketing and any topic we can bring value towards your audience, we will be delighted to be on, please email us back with more information. Cheers, Arman

What's wrong with this pitch?

- It doesn't use my name.
- It doesn't relate to my show.
- It doesn't share how or why the proposed topics relate to my audience or how they would bring value.
- It makes it all about them and not about me or my audience.
- There are no links or media kit.
- There is a mention of "value" but not what that value is.
- It doesn't say why John Doe would like to be a guest on my show.

## Example #2

Hi Michelle,

This is Judith. I am an assistant for John Doe, a CERTIFIED FINANCIAL PLANNER™, a three-time #1 Best Selling Author, the Owner of ABC Financial Services, a financial services firm in Chicago, Illinois, and co-host of the XYZ Podcast™. Over the years, he has helped hundreds of his clients take back control of their financial future and build their businesses with proven, tax-efficient financial solutions unknown to most financial gurus. He has become known as "The XYZ Financial Planner!"

John wanted me to reach out to you to see if you would be open to having him as a guest on your podcast to talk about financial solutions, income maximization, retirement, and more.

He is open to having a 15 minute introductory call to learn more about your podcast and how he can provide value to you and your audience.

Here are John's social media handles:

> His Website
> His Podcast
> His YouTube
> His LinkedIn
> His X
> His Facebook
> His Instagram
> His Book

John is a man on a mission to help you think differently about your money, your economy, and your future. After graduating with six figures of student loan debt and discovering a way to turn his debt into real wealth as he watched everybody lose their retirement savings and home equity in 2008, he knew that he needed to find a more predictable way to meet his financial objectives and those of his clients.

Please click on this link to schedule a 15 min appointment with John [*link to John's calendar*].

You can also directly schedule the podcast if you prefer to have the intro meeting during the podcast recording. Please choose the option for 50 minutes.

Please email me if you have any questions.

We look forward to hearing from you.

Thank you,
Judith

What's wrong with this pitch?

- My personal pet peeve is announcing your name when the email address tells me your name and you close the email with your signature line. That might be petty, but it's a fact.
- There is no relation to my show and no reason why John would be a good fit. Why did he ask you to reach out? I get that the entire pitch is about how great John is, but nowhere do you tell me how this will relate to my particular audience. Have you listened to my show? Probably not.
- Line items for each link made this a very long email to read. This is also all information that could have been (should have been) placed in an attached media kit.
- Telling me how to book an interview on my own show is snarky. I don't need to know that John is open to a call with me . . . he's asking to be a guest on MY show! I understand that Judith probably thought this would be a solution for me

to use, but all it does is show me John's free time instead of him taking that step to see what my availability is. Another red flag that this shouldn't be about you—it's about the host and the audience.

# BAD FOLLOW-UP EXAMPLES

> I bet you're busy, I just wanted to make sure that my previous email landed in your inbox.

Don't worry, it's in my inbox, but since the original pitch didn't include a single link and required me to do more homework (and you already said you know I'm busy!), it's been moved to the deleted folder. No, I didn't actually reply with that, but I sure thought it. You know the email landed in my inbox because the original didn't bounce back to you. The part about jumping to the top of your inbox as the reason for the follow-up is something that happens to even top journalists, so I know I'm not alone in my pet peeve of it.

## The *WORST* Three Follow-Up Emails I Have Ever Received

Here's email 1:

> Bing!

Here's email 2:

> Thoughts?

And here's email 3:

> Checking in!

I am not kidding when I include the above as the worst three follow-ups I have ever received. The worst one simply said "Bing!" This sender didn't only send this message once but did it again the following week. What infuriates me even more than the laziness in these follow-ups is that these all came from an agency that a client is paying money for. There's a lack of personalization and thought in these types of follow-up emails. Someone needed to check the follow-up off a to-do list, and this was the quickest way for the person to accomplish that task. Don't be this person.

Can we go back to "Bing!" for a moment? I know that's the sound that some inboxes make when you get a new email, but I'm still perplexed months after receiving this email why anyone would think that's appropriate or that it makes any sense. If you want people to take the time and make the effort to reply to you, then do the same in your follow-ups to them.

## WHAT'S THE HOST UP TO?

I don't say this to be discouraging, but the host isn't sitting at a desk waiting for your pitch email to hit the inbox. Most podcast hosts have full- or part-time jobs outside of their hosting duties. Podcast hosts might consider their shows a hobby, a creative outlet, a passion project, or an extension of their job or business. It's extremely rare for podcast hosts to have their show be their sole full-time job. I say all of this so that you understand that while you're emailing your pitches and sending follow-ups in addition to doing your everyday job and dealing with everyday life at home, the podcast hosts are working their normal jobs, and some might also be parenting, tending to household chores, etc. This is why providing as much relevant information as possible for the host is extremely important. Strive not to give the host homework. Be patient with your follow-ups because hosts are everyday people, like you. They take vacations, or have business trips, or have kid events to attend. You're dealing with human beings, so don't make this transactional. Make it personal!

---

## EXERCISE

### Send 10 Pitches, Wait Two Weeks, and Send a Follow-Up

You are already armed with your podcast pitch list, so now it's time to write your pitch emails. Follow the pitch blueprint below, and track your pitches on your Trello board.

1.  Subject line with your name included
    - ABC Podcast Guest—Your Name
2.  Friendly opening using the host's name
    - "Hi Joe" or "Good morning Joe"
3.  Episode you enjoyed and how you related to it, along with anything personal to the host
    - "I enjoyed listening to your podcast episode with [*insert guest's name*] about [*insert topic*]." Why did you like this episode? How did it resonate with you? What did you learn from it? "I wanted to reach out to you to introduce myself as a potential podcast guest because I'd love to share my knowledge on [*subject*] with your audience." Relate the topic to the show and why the audience would benefit from learning more from you, rather than someone else.
4.  Two or three sentences about you with your name hyperlinked to your website (mini bio)
    - "I am [*insert your title(s)*] with vast experience and knowledge on [*insert more generic topics*]." Hyperlink your website within this section.

5. Two or three topics from your media kit that you feel are the
   best fit for the show
   - "Since your podcast has a focus on [*insert topics or
     subjects*], I would love to share my experiences and
     expertise on: [*bullet-point two or three topics from your
     media kit*]."
6. A few places you've recently been interviewed that are
   hyperlinked to the actual interviews
   - "I've recently been interviewed on [*insert podcast shows
     with hyperlinks to your interviews and/or any other
     media outlets*]."
7. Friendly closing that says your media kit is also attached
8. "I've attached my media kit along with additional speaking
   topics that I am uniquely qualified to speak on. Please let me
   know if you have any questions at all."
9. Your name
   - "Thanks so much! [*your name*]"
10. Attach your media kit.

Notate your initial emails on your Trello board, and practice
being patient while you wait for replies to your pitch. If two to
three weeks go by without any further communication, check in
with the host via a concise and friendly follow-up email. Make
reference to the original email you sent so the host is armed
once again with all the relevant information.

Hi [*name*],

I'm following up on my email in regard to potentially
being a guest on your show. I'd love to further discuss
such an opportunity with you.

Thanks again!
[*your name*]

Don't forget to move your Trello card and notate the date you sent the first follow-up.

## SUMMARY

You've done it! You've sent your first set of pitches and are now ready for the interviews to begin. This can be one of the toughest parts emotionally because it is inevitable that you will be rejected. It's a part of sales, it's a part of life, and it's ultimately a part of putting yourself out there for speaking opportunities. Please don't get discouraged if you receive silence or a dreaded no thank you. If you get a no, then celebrate because your pitch was not only received but read as well. Keep in mind that there are millions of shows (quite literally) and you WILL receive that yes within weeks. If you don't, then it's time to look at the podcasts you are pitching to and ensure they are a good fit for your message and vice versa.

# 5

# HOMEWORK
# AS A GUEST

## PREPPING FOR YOUR INTERVIEW
## INVOLVES RESEARCH

I am a planner. I plan things out before I need to. Case in point, the other day I bought a new dress. When it arrived, I instantly knew that I would wear it to the next outdoor happy hour we would have with friends. It's long and orange with bright pink flowers. It screamed summer and happy, and it flowed when I walked. We don't even have a date on the calendar for the next happy hour, but I'm already preparing for it. This morning I texted my friend Cindy, asking if she and her husband wanted to come over for July 4th. Her response was yes, and she already knew what dessert she wanted to bring. Neither of us had plans set in stone, and yet we were both preparing for what we knew (or hoped) would be coming. Whether you've gotten a yes already or not, I want you to start preparing for your interviews as well.

I also want you to jump on the yes when you receive that email from the host! You don't have to be checking your inbox every 15 minutes, but when you do see that a host has replied, asking you to be a guest, and there's a calendar link included in it, you need to jump on it.

Interview prep isn't just about knowing all you can about the host and the show you're going to be on. Interview prep entails a lot of things you can and should do ahead of time to ensure that when it's go time, you just need to show up on time! Doing a lot of this preparation beforehand will also ensure that you will have to do less preparation for future interviews.

Some of the questions we will go over include:

- What will you bring to your interview?
- What will you wear?
- Where will you record?
- What platform will you be using?
- How do you best show up for a video podcast interview?
- What can you physically and mentally do to prepare for an interview?
- What types of interviews are there?

## DINNER PARTY PREPARATION

I shared with you how my friend Cindy and I were both preparing for events that weren't even confirmed yet, and with a dinner party, there is also preparation involved both before a date is made and even more so after the invitations have gone out. Whether we are talking about a dinner party, happy hour, Netflix and chill, birthday party, or potluck, the planning is all the same.

You start with a date, time, and place and then invite your guests. While you're waiting for your guests to RSVP, you're getting busy with a menu and possibly a theme for the dinner or party. I'm a big fan of trying to do the least amount of work the day of a party and during, so I like to prepare in advance. I'll create a menu, write up a grocery list, pick up some paper plates and napkins (if it's that kind of get-together), and decide on what kind of drinks to serve and what part of the house or backyard we'll have everyone gather in. And, of course, I need to decide on what I'll be wearing!

All these steps are what you'll be working on to get ready for your podcast interview, whether it's booked on your calendar yet or not. Preparation is a key component in a podcast interview because it ensures you show up professionally and as the expert you are. It's very obvious when someone hasn't taken the steps to be ready for an interview, and I'm not going to let that happen to you.

---

## BOOKING AN INTERVIEW TIME

Since I'm sharing all my secrets with you, I'm going to also share one of my biggest pet peeves. I cannot stand when I receive a pitch for a guest and I say yes to having the person be a guest on my show only to receive crickets back. Not a reply. No booking. Just pure silence. I don't understand if that's simply how our world now operates or if possibly the guest or the person pitching the guest decided that my show wasn't the right fit. If it's the latter reason, then neither person did good enough research to begin with. I certainly take that silence and file it away as a reminder for any future pitches from the sender and/or the potential guest. Don't ghost the host!

Most hosts will send you a link to their calendar or ask you for some potential dates and times you have available. Reply with a thank you and your availability as soon as you can. If the calendar link doesn't ask for your bio and headshot, then I preemptively include both those items with my email response. It's one less thing the host will need to ask you for and shows that you know what you're doing and are prepared!

If for some reason there are absolutely no dates and times that work for you, let the host know. If it's a really great fit, the host will definitely try to work with you. I have different calendars for different events.

Therefore, it might appear that I'm unavailable for podcast interviews at certain times, but if guests let me know what their schedule looks like, then oftentimes I will accommodate their schedule, especially when there are time zone differences.

## NEVER SHOW UP EMPTY-HANDED: HAVE A FREEBIE TO OFFER LISTENERS

I never show up empty-handed when I'm invited somewhere. My go-to is a bottle of wine, but you can never go wrong with flowers, candles, or something meaningful for your host. For your podcast interview, you're going to show up with a gift for the listening audience. Why? Because after listening to your interview, you want to make sure that you have a way to bring the listeners to your platform. You've already piqued their interest, hooked them in per se, and want to continue gaining their trust. Ultimately, you want them to see you as a familiar person they can count on and trust. To accomplish this, there are a few steps you will need to take first. This will be your call to action!

Most people have something free that they offer to people in exchange for subscribing to their newsletter. Politicians will ask for your email address so that you can follow along with their campaign or stay up to date on the issues that concern you. Coaches or service providers will ask for your email address in exchange for some tips or steps they've created that will help you while also further providing you with the knowledge they have, therefore, the hope is, steering you to work with them in the future. A wellness coach might offer mindset tips, or a sales coach might give out his verbiage for selling strategies. An author might send you sneak peaks of her upcoming book or invite you to be part of her book launch in exchange for your email address. It's exactly the same as when an online store asks for your email address so it can send you a coupon and thereby add you to its email list. The number of ways companies and people use to obtain your email address in exchange for something they offer you for free is truly endless.

You need to create something to offer to listeners so that they'll also share their email address with you. You will add these listeners to your email list and continue to gain their trust as you show them your expertise through your communications. The reason behind collecting email addresses is because they're a direct line to those listeners. You've earned their trust with what you shared on the podcast in exchange for even more knowledge that you're willing to share with them. You won't just need to give them something in return, but this is now your chance to allow them to get to know you even better by sending them weekly or monthly emails. You might also want to consider (if you haven't already) creating a welcome sequence email. This means that when people joins your list, a series of emails is sent to them automatically over time. They will get to know you, your business, your story, and more.

If you don't already have a freebie that someone can download, you can easily create one in Google Docs, Word, or Canva. Think about the questions people ask you over and over again and create a cheat sheet or tips that include your answers.

Here are some examples of free downloads I offer on my website:

- **Tips for being a great interviewer.** I offer tips on how to research a guest and prepare for the interview as well as best practices during the interview to ensure you are a great interviewer.
- **Podcast pitching checklist.** This is a cheat sheet that offers quick tips and tools on how to pitch yourself to podcasts. It's like a one-page overview of this book!
- **Podcast guest checklist.** You've landed the interview, but now you need to prepare. This is a quick tip sheet that offers tips on how to prepare for the interview and how to best show up as a guest, along with a reminder on ways to thank your host.

Notice that these are all areas that I'm known for and an expert in. I'm often asked how to be a great guest, and oftentimes hosts ask me what the secret is to being a great interviewer. I decided that since I've been asked often enough, I'd jot down some tips and put them in a pretty document via Canva. I ensured that the look and feel aligned with my branding (color and font, logo, headshot, and bio). People are free to download the tips in exchange for their email address. I utilize a service called Flodesk to manage my email list and downloads, but you can also use Mailchimp, Active Campaign, Sprout Social, or a number of other email list services. When people add their email to my list, they receive the download and then are automatically added to my welcome sequence of emails that share how I got started, what some of my favorite podcast episodes are, and what kind of work I do. These emails are in addition to the weekly ones I send to my entire list.

My business is to pitch clients to be on podcasts, so you might be wondering why I'd provide anyone a cheat sheet for free. It goes back to when I heard Amy Porterfield say that you should give really good knowledge away for free. The people who hear what you have to offer will be thinking that if you give such great stuff away for free, imagine what they would get if they paid for your services! Your freebie shouldn't be a place where you skimp on what you know. Don't be afraid to show listeners that you are an expert. I have given out checklists that offer quite a bit of detail because I want people to understand that I know what I'm talking about and they can trust me. Heck, look at everything that's provided in this book! Does it mean some readers can replicate what I do? Possibly. Am I worried about that? No, because they aren't me, and no one can do exactly what I do, the way I do it. On top of that, I've been building relationships for years with hosts and with my clients. If I lived my life in fear of others taking business away from me, then I'd be miserable . . . and my business would suffer.

In addition to the tips and tools you're going to offer, make sure that your logo, biography, and contact information are all included. This is another great way to ensure that the people who heard you and liked you enough to visit your website and give you their email address to download your tips know exactly who you are and how to contact you. There would be nothing worse than for them to download valuable information from you, refer to it, and then forget your name or business because it's nowhere to be found on your download. I also include my headshot so that I become a familiar face to them.

Another tip is that this is something you can put on your website permanently. It doesn't have to only be something you give out when you're on a show being interviewed. Share it with your followers on social media too! It's a great way to build your email list!

## CLOTHES THAT MAKE YOU FEEL CONFIDENT

Now that you're armed with a gift, let's talk about what you're going to wear to the party . . . I mean the interview! Have you ever owned a "power suit"? When I worked in the corporate world, I certainly did. Now, I have power tops, because when you're doing a podcast interview, even if it's video, no one is going to know what kind of bottoms you are wearing, so feel free to be comfortable. A power suit or power top is going to be clothing that makes you feel good. You put it on and feel confident. It might be the color, the style, or the fit that does the trick for you. For me, a top that is blue (any shade!) or emerald green is my go-to. You don't want to have something that doesn't fit right, or you'll want to keep adjusting. Be comfortable and confident, because it's going to shine through during your interview.

Some tips on the clothing you should wear for your interview:

- Wear what is weather appropriate for wherever you are. You don't want to wear something that is going to make you sweat and be uncomfortable.
- Avoid stripes and polka dots. You might think they're fun, but they can also be distracting and sometimes distorted on camera.
- Go for a solid color that complements your skin tone and eyes.

- Quick tips from InStyle:
  - For warm skin tones, go for orange, yellow, or even gold. Bright colors are also good, along with natural earth tones such as browns, deep tonal reds, and rich shades of green.
  - For cool skin tones, stick with charcoal, cool blues, and violet. You can also utilize pastels, such as pale blues and pinks, soft yellow, or light green.
- You know what looks good on you … it's that color that people always give you a compliment about how it brings out the color of your eyes or somehow makes you appear to be glowing. Wear that!

When it comes to jewelry, I'm one who loves a statement piece or something that complements my top—but in this case, subtle is best. You should be wearing headphones, so there's no need to focus on your earrings, especially if they dangle. Avoid wearing bangle bracelets or anything that makes noise when you move (this includes earrings) or, say, you rest your wrist on your desk. Try testing this out before the interview. You might be wearing a necklace that you didn't think made any noise, but suddenly it's all the microphone seems to pick up because every time you move, the necklace and your shirt rub together. Also be aware of your hair. If you have longer hair and are wearing a shirt with a collar, the sound of you moving your hair over your shoulder can sometimes be heard during the recording. Do as much as you can to have the least amount of distractions. Yes, this does seem to be very detailed, but I have heard interviews be ruined because of hair swaying and jewelry clanking.

Remember that not all podcasts will have a video component, so this preparation step won't always apply. Most hosts will let you know if video is used and whether or not it will be released. If you aren't sure, then just ask!

# PODCAST RECORDING PLATFORMS

Before you jump on a call with someone, you normally check your calendar to see how the call will take place, right?! You should do the same prior to your podcast interviews. There are a number of podcast recording platforms, and it's important to know what kind of tech is necessary for each one. The hosts will tell you beforehand what platform they are utilizing and whether or not there will be a video component. If you aren't sure, simply ask them. It's a very common question. Some hosts will utilize video just to be able to see you, but none of the video recorded will be released to the public. If this is the case, you should still show up in a professional manner. This is also a great opportunity to take some behind-the-scenes selfies together to help promote the episode, so it's best to avoid the "I just rolled out of bed" look!

Some of the most common software platforms that podcast hosts record with are listed below. I've included tips for each of them. In most cases, it's best to ensure your computer is able to access these platforms ahead of time. This might require downloading software in advance, or it might be that you can only utilize a specific browser, in which case it should be updated as well. In ALL cases, I suggest you use an external microphone and headphones. Not to worry—I have some suggestions for them as well! Another tip that is common for almost all of the platforms is that you will be provided with a link to click on to join the interview. If you haven't used the platform before, you will be asked to allow it to use your microphone and camera. The link is most commonly found in the calendar invite, but some hosts will email it separately to you.

Now, as promised, here are some of the most common software platforms that podcast hosts record with:

- Zoom
  - It's best if you create a free account, because then you can include your name and the profile picture associated with

you. The platform will ask you to download its client, and it has unique ones depending on your operating system.

- Zoom allows for video and/or audio recording.
- Zencastr
    - Zencastr is simply a website with nothing necessary to download.
    - The platform has to be accessed from a laptop or desktop computer.
    - It is only supported by Google Chrome, Microsoft Edge, and Brave.
    - Zencastr allows the host to select audio recording, audio and video recording, or audio recording with a video component.
- Riverside
    - Riverside has a livestream component if the host wants to stream your interview on Facebook, etc.
    - It uses Google Chrome.
    - It has a video component.
    - It has a "green room" that you will enter prior to the host allowing you access to the "studio."
- StreamYard
    - You must utilize a laptop or desktop computer.
    - It is only compatible with Google Chrome or Firefox.
    - It has a video component.
- SquadCast
    - SquadCast supports all browsers.
    - It has a video component.

## WHERE SHOULD YOU RECORD YOUR INTERVIEWS?

For years I recorded in my walk-in closet, sitting behind a TV dinner tray table. I have had clients who recorded under a comforter in a hotel room. Others have recorded in the car. You can literally record anywhere, but the biggest thing to keep in mind is to ensure your sound is absorbed and not echoing or bouncing off empty walls. Clothes and comforters can help absorb the sound! I know that not everyone has a walk-in closet to record in, but with some prep ahead of time, you can record from home and sound like a pro!

The key to sounding like you're in a professional studio is to test out various locations in your home and make sure your sound isn't bouncing off walls. Choose a room that has no or near-to-no reflections or echo. A good rule is if you clap and hear the reflections, you may want to choose a better room. Record yourself in different rooms and in different areas of the rooms, and play it back to see what sounds best.

What are you going to use to record? You're serious about podcast interviews and want to present yourself as not only an expert but a professional as well. I suggest purchasing an external microphone instead of using the one that is built into your computer. Below is a list of microphones my editor and I recommend to clients (the prices are accurate at the time of writing—but perhaps not at the time of your reading—so you'll need to double-check them). I also suggest buying a pop filter to help with the sound.

- Blue Yeti ($130)
  - I use the Blue Yeti microphone. The one difference with this mic is that you speak into the side of it and NOT on the top! If you get this mic, PLEASE remember this tip when using it!
- TONOR Computer Cardioid Condenser PC Gaming Mic ($42.99, but normally on sale for $29.99 on Amazon)
  - I gift this microphone to all my clients, AND it comes with a pop filter and stand.
- Rode NT-USB ($120)
- Audio-Technica AT2020USB-X ($129)
- Apogee MIC Plus USB ($260)
- Pop filter ($8)

Additionally, you can purchase a soundproof foaming shield that can either protect just your microphone or take up some space on your desk. This is usually less than $40 but not what I would consider a "must-have." You can also hang towels or blankets in the area as a free alternative. If you do decide to record in the closet, do so in the middle! Going into a corner traps the immediate sound reflections causing the recording to sound boxy or like you're in a helmet.

Once you have your mic set up, try out some practice recordings in different spots. Play the audio back and listen to what sounds best. Test out your settings to make sure your microphone isn't set too low. Whatever you do, don't be afraid to test things out. By testing and being prepared, you're going to ensure you show up confident and ready for your interview. The last thing you want is to be distracted by technical difficulties!

## LET'S TALK VIDEO

Some podcasts will have a video component, and you'll need to show up camera-ready! In most cases, your built-in camera will work, or you can use an external camera that you already have. Also, be sure your background isn't too distracting. Behind me I have my diplomas and a neutral-color wall. Bookshelves or a nice painting is also great to have in the background. If you aren't sure about your background, check out Room Rater on X. This account rates the backgrounds of people who are interviewed on the news and elsewhere. It's not just comedic—it gives you some great tips on what you should and shouldn't have for a background—like a bunch of wires going in different directions is a no-no.

A tip for looking your best is to try to be in a room with natural lighting, such as you facing a window. An alternative if you don't have great lighting is a ring light that you can buy on Amazon for under $30. One tip for a ring light is that if you wear glasses, make sure the ring light isn't reflecting on your glasses. I share this because just the other night on the news, the person interviewed was in his home, and the ring light image was on both the lenses of his glasses. It was distracting and noticeable. You can test this out by opening a Zoom video without anyone else on the call and check out what's looking back at you. I can't emphasize enough the importance of testing each of these elements. Not only will these testing tips come in handy for your podcast interviews, but if you have any other types of meetings or interviews in the future, these tips are relevant!

## GETTING PREPARED MENTALLY AND PHYSICALLY

Now that you are technologically ready, it's time to get your emotions and mindset in check. Your nerves might be a bit jittery those first couple of interviews, and that's completely normal and natural. Some of the world's greatest speakers still get nervous before going on stage. Quite honestly, my opinion is that if you aren't nervous, then something isn't right. I can talk all day long about podcasts, pitching, my life story, and more, and yet I still get the flutters in my stomach before I dive in. A big part of this stems from the fact that you're about to talk to someone who is basically a stranger and aren't quite sure what questions the person will be asking you. Preparation is such a big key to finding confidence and eliminating interview nerves, which is why I am talking so much about being prepared. Let's talk about how to get ready to alleviate as many of those butterflies as possible.

Before you think I'm getting all "woo-woo" on you, know that I'm not someone who regularly meditates, does breathwork, or practices yoga, BUT I do know those things can and do make a difference in my body and mind when I do any of them. Consider doing a meditation before your interview to get your head in the right space. Breathwork is a great calming and recentering exercise you can do before an interview. You can download the Calm or Peloton app to find a meditation or just google it! YouTube offers amazing free videos on meditation and breathwork and more!

Start the night before with a good night's sleep. The night before is not the time to head out for an epic happy hour that leaves you dehydrated and with a hoarse voice. Speaking of hydration, be sure to drink plenty of water beforehand and stay hydrated during your interview. I always have a glass of water with me during an interview as well. *A word of caution:* Make sure the cup you use won't make a clanking sound if you put it down after taking a sip. Another random tidbit is to not have a glass container with a metal straw to drink from. I mention this because I've heard it happen, and it's extremely noticeable.

You've been prepping for days, but there's still more prep to do on the day of your interview.

Prior to your interview starting:

- Put your phone in airplane mode.
- Turn off all notifications—make sure that your texts and calls don't come through your computer and that your emails do not "ding" a notification.
- Try to keep the dog from barking and the kids from screaming.
  - We all get that this is a normal part of life and it happens, but do your best to ensure that someone isn't knocking on your door throughout the interview.
- Know which platform your interview will be on and ensure that you have the latest version of whatever is needed to join via the link sent to you.

## PREPPING FOR YOUR TOPIC

In addition to finding a relaxed state to be in, you should also prepare what you're going to be speaking on. Did the host select one of your topics from your media kit? Is this an interview about your journey on how you got to where you are? Did the host provide questions ahead of time? Consider what you know or think you know about the upcoming interview and what you will want to say. At a certain point, you're going to have your spiel down. You'll probably have a handful of examples to go along with your story and messaging, which we'll be discussing in the next chapter. Being armed with what you're going to talk about also helps alleviate any kind of nervousness that might be coming up for you. Don't be afraid to jot down notes on a Post-it and put them up where you can see them but the host can't. It's more than OK to give yourself a cheat sheet in order to remember important things.

Before you go into the interview, please listen to an episode or two if you haven't already (but you already should have before you pitched the show!). Some hosts will literally end every show asking the same exact question to their guest. I remember a podcast production client of mine who did this. Her question was, if a movie was made about your life, which movie star would play you? I had listened to every single episode of hers and could always tell when guests were shocked or surprised by the question because they'd never listened to her show before. Here's the kicker though: When she interviewed me, I'd completely forgotten that she would be asking me the question. Since I'd listened to every episode she'd recorded, I had already considered this question, so I was prepared to answer it, but it did slip my mind in the moment.

Hosts usually have an interview style, and if you listen to the questions they ask, they might be repetitive to a certain extent. I was prepping a client last summer for a big podcast interview she had booked. It was her first interview, and she was very well known in her industry, so she wanted to make sure she nailed this interview. We set up a series of mock interviews together, and in order for me to properly interview her, I listened to a number of interviews the host had previously done with other guests. When I asked her what her favorite Asian dish was to make and eat, she was shocked. She thought that was completely off topic and stopped me. Evidently she hadn't been listening to all the interviews the host did because it was a question he asked in the middle of every single interview! Preparation is key! Of course it's even better if someone will do a mock interview with you, but simply listening to past episodes will help you in this area immensely.

My interview style is conversational, but I do a lot of homework on the people I'm interviewing prior to the interview. I will ask guests about things I read in their book or online about them, and sometimes what I ask comes as a surprise to them. Not because it wasn't public or common knowledge, but because I took the time to dig a bit deeper into who they are. Do the same for your host! It definitely goes a long way when you can hold up your end of the conversation by relating to the host. A great example of doing amazing research prior to an interview occurred as I was writing this book. I interviewed *New York Times* bestselling author Eve Rodsky. I'd done my research on her, but I certainly wasn't prepared for her to have done so much research about me. She'd listened to my past episodes and used what she learned about me to share how I was able to find and utilize my "unicorn space." Knowing that we both came prepared and were invested even before the interview started made our conversation more intimate and thoughtful. Show your guests this kind of thoughtfulness, and I promise you that your interviews will be even more amazing than you could have ever expected.

## THE KEYS TO BEING AN EFFECTIVE COMMUNICATOR

In most cases you won't know the questions the host is going to ask you in advance, but that's not always the rule of thumb. Some hosts provide standard questions that every guest is asked, some hosts will ask the guest to provide questions for them to ask, and others will simply want to converse as if you were meeting for coffee. The good part is that regardless of which of these formats a host goes with, you'll know ahead of time and can prepare properly. The key will then be to effectively communicate your expertise.

To be the most effective communicator, you should follow the five Cs of communication: Be clear, cohesive, complete, concise, and concrete. These communication skills will come in handy not only in podcast interviews but in all speaking that you do:

- **Clear/clarity.** Be clear about your message and what you're trying to convey. We know you are an expert in your field, but try not to use vocabulary that only you or someone in your industry is familiar with. Various fields are filled with acronyms that not everyone knows. This was very true when I was in aviation . . . heck, in that industry the entire alphabet has designated words for each letter! Let people understand what you're saying by ensuring you understand it as well.
- **Cohesive.** Do your best not to mix ideas or stories that don't fit together. You shouldn't confuse listeners with what your story or expertise is. If you have a story that goes with your topic, make sure they flow together.
- **Complete.** Give listeners the overall picture. Don't leave details out about why something is the way it is or why the outcome of your story is important. This isn't a time to hoard your knowledge or experience. Give listeners all the details while also ensuring they want to learn more from you. Compare it with going on a first date. You went to dinner and had a lot of fun getting to know the person, to the point that you'd like to learn even more about your date.
- **Concise.** Nobody likes a rambler. Don't draw the conversation out longer than it needs to be. Don't try to add filler just because you can. It'll detract from your overall message and story.
- **Concrete.** Don't be vague when you're talking. Be as specific as possible. For example, saying you work is vague, but saying you are a podcast publicist is concrete. It allows the listener to truly understand what you are referring to and gets your message across more clearly.

## SHOWING UP AS YOU

The most important part of a podcast interview is for you to show up as yourself. This is not a time to pretend to be someone else or who you think the host might want you to be. YOU landed this interview. It's YOUR knowledge, expertise, and message that the host wants to share with listeners. Please bring that energy and your genuine self to the interview. There's no need to act differently than who you are, no need to wear makeup if you don't normally or be someone you're not. Remember that you are the only you in the world, and that is who needs to show up to your interviews.

We all know our own pet peeves, insecurities, and what some might call faults within ourselves. One of my biggest issues with any presentation or public speaking is that I start off talking too fast. I've always been this way since I was a child doing the readings at Sunday mass. My mom always reminded me to slooooooow down. I had to tell myself not to look at her, because otherwise I'd catch her mouthing what I should be doing and get distracted. These days I've found new ways to remind myself without causing any distraction to myself. I can feel it in my body when my heart rate is increased and I'm barely taking a breath in between words. Honestly, I even get a bit sweaty (sorry for the TMI!). If you've done any kind of public speaking, you know exactly what I'm talking about. So what do I do about it? I take a breath and remind myself to slow down and take my time. There is no reason to rush through your story or message. Take the listener and host on your journey with you. The key is to be as natural as possible, so if you have to say "Whew! I'm sorry I'm talking fast; let me slow things down a bit," then know that's fine. It shows that you're human just like everyone else. I promise you that with experience under your belt, you will naturally slow down and become more comfortable.

In the next chapter, we'll discuss what it takes to be a great storyteller. My biggest hint is that to be a great storyteller, you need to be yourself. Don't be afraid of what people might think about you because it's really none of your business. I'm sure you've heard that saying before, and it's the truth. What people think of you is simply what they think. It shouldn't affect who or what you are, because those opinions and thoughts are really about the person whose head they reside in. Your business is to ensure you are sharing everything you can with the host and audience. You have a unique gift that needs to be shared. No, not everyone will be your fan, nor is everyone meant to be. Just as some people prefer Coke over Pepsi (unless you're me and it's Pepsi over Coke), your messaging will resonate with some, but not with others, and that's OK.

## WHAT'S THE HOST UP TO?

Just as you've been busy prepping for your interview, the host has as well. The host is looking at your social media, reading your bio, checking out your website, reading your book, and doing homework on who you are and what you do. Some hosts will write down questions they want to ask you, while others will simply allow the conversation to guide itself. For my show, I read every page of a book that a guest has written. In addition, I read the guest's bio and stalk his or her website and social media channels. I don't come up with questions ahead of time, but by having done so much research on my guest, I have an idea of what I want to ask about—the parts of the book I'd like to dive further into, the things that stuck out at me when I read through the guest's website, and more. In preparation, hosts also ensure they're properly set up with what they need for the interview by being hydrated, free of distractions, and ready to go with their software platforms.

## EXERCISE

### Create a Freebie and Get Your Setup Ready

Create a freebie that is filled with tips and tools that you can share with the audience. Tie the freebie to your email list service so that people can give you their email address in exchange for your download. If you don't have a service set up, then it's time to find one. My recommendation is Flodesk, and you can get 50 percent off if you go through this site: https://flodesk.com/c/MING1D.

Go back through the steps we discussed and think about the top questions you are asked most frequently. Create a cheat sheet in Canva or a software of your preference. Don't forget to include your contact details and brand them to reflect your website. Save this as a PDF file so that it can be uploaded to your email list software and easily downloaded by your followers.

This next exercise is going to be fun . . . get your interview area set up, and get ready to hit "Record"! Purchase a microphone and start testing out where your sound is best. Turn your camera on and look at your background. Is it too distracting? How's your lighting? Consider how you'd feel if you had to record an interview tomorrow. Does the thought make you nervous? If so, I want you to look up a meditation or breathwork exercise on YouTube. Duarte, Inc., has a great five-minute calming meditation that is specifically designed for pre-presentations (*A Short Meditation before Public Speaking*; https://www.youtube.com/watch?v=UuWAi9vAMkE).

Here's a checklist you can use to ensure you're fully prepared for your interview:

- Create a downloadable freebie.
- Connect the download to your email list service.
- Purchase an external microphone.
- Perform test recordings in different locations.
- Select your recording location and check the lighting.
- Purchase a ring light if there isn't enough natural light where you'll be recording.
- Listen to an episode or two of the podcast you'll be on.
- Look up the host who is interviewing you.

- Test the platform (or at least know what platform if you've already used it) to ensure you don't need to download something and restart your computer.
- Get a good night's sleep.
- Choose a top to wear that has a good color to complement your skin tone and eyes.
- Remove any loud jewelry.
- Drink water.
- Turn off notifications.
- Put your phone in airplane mode.
- Get rid of any distractions.
- Do a quick meditation or breathwork exercise.

## SUMMARY

Friend, you are ready to record your first interview, and not only that, you're ready to grow your email list! You look and sound like a professional. You've calmed all those butterflies, and you're distraction-free. Some of these tips might sound like common sense, but you'd be surprised how many people don't remember to take these steps to ensure they sound professional and aren't distracted by an email or text message. The more prepared you are, the more relaxed and comfortable you'll be when it's time to record.

# LIGHTS, CAMERA, ACTION!

## BEING A STORYTELLER THAT WILL WOW THE HOST *AND* LISTENERS

Storytelling is an artform, but I believe anyone can learn and master it. I've seen courses advertised on how to become a good storyteller, and honestly, they make me cringe because you don't need to pay money for a course to learn how to be a good storyteller. You simply need to tell your story with genuine authenticity, great anecdotes, and direction. Don't worry though. I'll go into further detail about what that actually means as you continue to read. The main point that I want you to understand is that you already have what it takes to be a great storyteller on podcasts. I wholeheartedly believe that, because only you can tell your own story.

Being a perfect podcast guest isn't just about knowing how to tell your story; it's also about engaging with the host. It's not simply answering questions, but actually having a meaningful conversation, one that is a give-and-take. When the conversation isn't two-way, it can become awkward. I was interviewing a journalist who was quite obviously more comfortable with being the interviewer than the interviewee. With her background being in the art of asking the questions, she wasn't fully prepared when I replied with a statement instead of just firing off another question. I was conversing with her, but she had a different definition of "interview" since the ones she'd always been on the other side of were simply question and answer. She thought I should be feeding questions, she'd provide me with the answers, and then I'd move on without further commentary. That's not a conversation, nor is it my personal interview style. For interviewers, this is what separates a good interview from a great one ... when you do more than simply offer a Q&A. This is what communication is all about. It's the true definition of what conversation means. To have a great conversation, you should also spend some time getting to know who you will be talking to—preparation is key! It's like looking up directions to the house party before you actually start driving the car!

A podcast interview is a place where you're also going to share freely of your knowledge. Remember in Chapter 5 when I mentioned you should give away your expertise in your freebie freely? You should be doing it even more so in the interview. This is your chance to let the audience not only know what you know, but get to know you on a deeper and more intimate level.

Lastly, as any good guest does, you're going to thank your host. Outside of simply saying thank you, I'll share ways that go even further than those two powerful words that are so often forgotten.

## WHO GETS THE COVETED INVITE FOR YOUR HAPPY HOUR?

As a party host, what do the perfect guests look like to you? My perfect guests show up on time or fashionably late within 15 minutes, and they have something to contribute to the evening that works as a preemptive thank you, like a bottle of wine, or flowers, or a dish to share. They haven't brought unexpected guests with them and are excited to share an evening or afternoon by the pool with you. They are ready to engage in conversation with the stories we share and catch up on what's been happening to ultimately turn our day into something we don't want to end. The next day, we are texting each other to say what a great time it was and how grateful we are to have gotten together. We might exchange pics from the event and relive some of the hilarious highlights.

A lot of the same qualities of a great party guest are the same as a great podcast guest. It's about being a present person, one who is willing to engage in conversation and who is also grateful for the opportunity to be welcomed into your home. Take a moment to consider what your definition of a great guest is and consider what qualities that entails.

## WHO IS YOUR HOST?

One of the best ways to get rid of any nerves prior to your interview is to get to know your host. You most likely won't get an opportunity for a deep conversation before your interview, and logging on to record might actually be the first time you even speak to each other. Some hosts might ask for a pre-interview, in which case you will get to chat with them for 20 minutes or so before booking your actual interview date. The incredible invention of social media and the internet allows you to get to know just about anyone without ever having to speak to the person. Not only this, but the host has a podcast and is literally handing you the knowledge of the host AND the guests on a silver platter with past episodes! I'm always amazed at how much background information I can find on people. One of my favorite (and probably annoying) things to do when watching old movies on TCM is to google the actors or actresses and spout off everything I find intriguing about them to my husband. I love facts about when they were born or died, if the dates have something in common with another event, how many spouses they had, and what their upbringing was like, along with how they died and where they're buried. It's fascinating to be able to get to know people just by googling them. You can do this for more than just movie stars. Everyone is googleable!

Your first step in getting to know who your host is, is to simply go to the person's website. Read the About page. You'd be surprised how often people overlook this somewhat obvious step. The website owner is literally spoon-feeding you background information! I've landed interviews for clients and myself by simply reading the About page of a host and mentioning similarities between us or what I found fascinating about the person's story. It means a lot to people to know that you've made an effort and taken that step to show you not only care but are genuinely interested in who they are. There's no reason to make this more complicated than it needs to be, and every podcast I've ever pitched to has a website and will tell you about the host, so please do this bare minimum. You can expect this to be done in return prior to your interview as well.

Googling people to learn more about them also lets you peek into where they've been, what they've done, and what their goals might be. Check out some of the interviews they've done on other shows. Do they have a book out? Read the back cover or the summary on Amazon to see what it's about. Don't forget that this is exactly what every journalist or publicist would also be doing to you to get to know you ... as a client or as a reliable source.

By taking these simple steps, you now have more to talk about with your host and some talking points that might be able to bring up in your conversation that relates to your story or message. It's powerful to be able to show that you took time to get to know people before meeting them, and it also shows that you genuinely care about the interview. You aren't simply showing up for yourself and what you can get out of the hour together, but you're reciprocating the effort and time the host is putting into speaking with you. Hey, your authenticity is showing!

Why is all of this important? Because most people don't do it, and YOU aren't most people. I am not most people. If you come on my show, then rest assured that I will know as much as I possibly can about you before we even say hello. I will have read your book from cover to cover, no skimming. If you are my client, I will have done the same thing before our first one-to-one meeting. I'll also have googled you and stalked your social media accounts, so beware! It surprises me that this is so rare since this is an everyday practice for me.

I interviewed a woman in the book industry who had just published a book of her own. She complimented me on my interview questions because it was very obvious that I had actually read her book. I commented that, of course, I had read her book and didn't she read all the books of her clients as well? Her answer was . . . no. She admitted to me that she'd probably be much better at her job if she did read all her clients' books. As someone whose job it is to promote other people, I don't know how you could possibly promote someone if you didn't know all the ins and outs related to the person. I already said that I'm not all people, so maybe this is simply my personal approach to PR and my commitment to my clients, but I think it should be everyone's approach when it comes to interviews and promotions.

If you aren't consuming as much information on a person that is literally gifted to you, then you're missing out. You can't truly connect with another human if the interest is one-sided. This is the truth no matter what the relationship is between you and someone else, whether it's personal or professional. If one side isn't into the other, then it's just not going to work. The same can be said for a podcast interview. It's very obvious when one person shows he wants to be where he is in the moment and the other person isn't as interested. Think of it just as you would dating. You know when someone wishes she could be anywhere on the planet except for the current spot she is taking up space in. The person doesn't want to be at the dinner table with you in the restaurant. She doesn't really want to hear how your day went or how Aunt Susie is recovering from her bunion. Oh, was that a yawn you just saw? You don't want others to think you're THAT person. You want people to see how engaged you are and that you're really into not only the topic but the conversation you're having. Remember the book and movie *He's Just Not That into You*? Don't be the "he."

To help with conversation flow and to ensure there's no lull, I find that being armed with conversation points outside of my topic(s) helps me be more relaxed. Humanizing another person makes the person more accessible. I read Meaghan B. Murphy's book *Your Fully Charged Life: A Radically Simple Approach to Having Endless Energy and Filling Every Day with Yay* and wanted to interview her on my show. Meaghan is the editor in chief of *Woman's Day* magazine and can be seen on the *Today* show quite often. To me, she's a pretty big deal and an overall fun and full-of-life woman. I read her book entirely before pitching to her and was saddened to learn that her father passed away from pancreatic cancer. My father also passed away from pancreatic cancer when I was seven years old. When I emailed Meaghan asking if she'd be a guest on my show, I let her know that I'd read and enjoyed her book. I also included the mention of my father passing away from the same nasty cancer that her father had. Meaghan graciously came on my show and during the interview mentioned that one of the reasons she wanted to meet me was because our fathers both had pancreatic cancer and felt it connected us. Wow! Please, please, please see this as absolute proof that when you genuinely share of yourself, you are connecting with the person on the other side of the email. I was vulnerable when I shared that with Meaghan, but she'd also been vulnerable in sharing her own story with all her readers. Being authentically you will be what people feel and be the true reason why they want to interview you and learn more about you.

Whether you are pitching yourself, are prepping for an interview, or are the host looking for guests, go that extra mile to show your human side and relate to the other person. In sharing yourself, it allows others to share themselves with you and be more open. It creates a comfortable and trusting atmosphere and shows others that they're not alone in whatever they're going through. This is the intimacy of a podcast and the way lives are changed.

# THE ANATOMY OF
# A PERFECT PODCAST GUEST

Now that you've thought about what your definition of a great guest is, what do you think goes into being a perfect podcast guest? I'll share with you what my perfect podcast guest is like. My description of a dream podcast guest might seem very detailed, because it is, but I'm sharing with you a proven checklist that will ensure you are the perfect guest if you follow my criteria:

- **Be punctual.** It starts with someone who shows up on time. A podcast interview is NOT the moment to be fashionably late! Being right on time at the very minute the interview begins is absolutely fine, but please don't be late. The number one reason guests turn up tardy is because they didn't know they needed to download or update their software in order to utilize the recording platform, or they simply weren't familiar with what browser they would need to use (even if this was provided in the instructions). Research the recording platforms I've mentioned, and ensure you know what platform the host is going to use. This is information that is always provided to a guest, in either the email or the calendar invitation.

- **Be distraction-free.** What do you think when people you're having a conversation with keep checking their phone or looking at the time? They're distracted by something, and even though it might not be their intention, it comes off that they just don't want to be where they are at that moment ... with you. It's rude and off-putting. When you're a podcast guest, turn off your notifications and put your phone in airplane mode. We live in a time where many of us work from home with partners, kids, and pets. Hosts understand that there might be an interruption, but let those you live with know that you're going to be recording an interview and to please not disturb you for 30 to 60 minutes. Not all hosts have editors for their shows, or they are the editor in addition to being the host. Having to notate during an interview (or during the editing process) when a phone rang or someone walked in is a nuisance. It takes up more time, and quite frankly if it's something that could have been prevented, then it's simply rude. Some podcast editors might even charge more to look for those types of edits; therefore, you could be costing the host more money by not being fully present. I have actually been able to hear a guest typing on a computer while recording an interview with me. You don't need to have an interview with video to know when someone isn't fully present! Show up! Block the time on your calendar and be present. This is as much for the host as it is for you, the guest. Listeners will also be able to hear distractions that can't be edited, and it'll be an immediate reflection of who you are.

- **Be camera-ready.** If you aren't sure if the interview will be video, simply ask. Consider how you are showing up and if being in a tank top with a messy bun or looking like you are the founder of a cryptocurrency company is appropriate or not. I'm not a makeup person, so don't feel like you need to get your *Real Housewives* glam squad over, but do your best to look presentable. You should have already scouted out and found your best-sounding and -looking location to record, so that shouldn't be an issue. Remember that I recorded audio and video interviews for years in my walk-in closet. I always made sure I tidied up a bit and folded or hung clothes before going on camera though!

- **Know where the interview is.** When you go to a new location, you normally check a map for directions and drive time, so you should have done the same thing prior to your interview. You wouldn't jump in the car five minutes before the party and then check traffic, so don't do that with a podcast interview. What recording platform are you using?

Have you used it before? Are your mic and camera plugged in and working (just like checking for gas in your car)?

- **Hydrate.** Make sure you're hydrated, and keep a glass of water nearby in case you are suddenly parched from so much talking. When COVID hit and I talked less to people, my voice became hoarse much more quickly than before. Stay hydrated!

## THE ANATOMY OF A GREAT STORYTELLER

Have you noticed that there's a new buzzword that pops up every couple of years? For a long time in the corporate world, it was all about "synergy," and then everyone was "leaning in." The current buzzword, whether you're in the corporate world, nonprofit sector, or just about anywhere, is "storytelling." I have seen courses launched on how to be a good storyteller. You'll find a MasterClass, TED Talks, *Forbes* articles, and books on the very topic of storytelling—and they all say the same thing. I'm going to save you a lot of time and money because I'll share with you what all these platforms say storytelling is and how to be a great storyteller, and then I'm going to let you know the exact steps it takes for YOU to be an incredible storyteller.

This general overview comes from a MasterClass article, "How to Become a Great Storyteller," that says in order for you to become a great storyteller, you need to:

- Make it personal.
- Know your story.
- Know your audience.
- Don't give it all away at once.
- Have an element of surprise.
- Get outside of your comfort zone.

These are great tips, but how do you do all this AND be a great storyteller? These tips are important ones to keep in mind, but there's a lot more that goes into telling a story or ensuring you can garner someone's vote or educate people on why your cause is important and needs attention paid to it. You've not only got to pull the members of your audience in, but keep them there, paying attention and wanting to know what's next.

The first step in being a good storyteller is that you know why you are sharing the story, wanting the interview, and wanting to speak on your particular topic. What is your motivation behind all of this? Why is your topic/story important? What makes you the right person to be interviewed on all of this? These are all questions we answered in Chapter 1 around your topics, so you should already be able to answer these questions. Knowing your why is going to help you during your introduction of yourself and what you're going to talk about.

What's your end goal? What do you want to gain from the interviews? Do you want the vote of the listeners in an upcoming election? Are you trying to gain volunteers for your cause or advocates who will also work toward achieving the goal you are working toward? Do you want people to buy your book or to create a launch team for it? Are you looking for more clients for your product or service? Knowing what you want and who your audience is will allow you to home in on your messaging based on the targets you are trying to reach. Something to keep in mind is that the podcast audiences you are pitching to should already align with your target audience, meaning that your storytelling techniques shouldn't be changing much from one interview to the next. If your target audience includes women, you certainly won't be pitching yourself to and interviewing on podcasts that are solely for men. This goes for any target audience and is an important factor to consider. We speak differently to different audiences. That's just a fact. If you keep changing your audience, then your story and the way you tell it will need to be changed just as often. It's pretty safe to say that your target audience isn't going to fluctuate greatly; therefore, your storytelling abilities should also remain the same.

Knowing your end goal is going to help you keep focus and on track. There's nothing worse than someone who drags on telling a story and you're left wondering when the person is going to get to the point or how it relates to the topic at hand. If you haven't already written out your end goals, do so now. Look at each of your speaking topics and figure out how they relate to your goal. How can you tie the two together, and what stories or examples should be tied in for each topic in order to reach that goal?

One of the most important aspects of a good storyteller is being consistent. Consistency is a trait that I feel is important not only in storytelling but in life overall. Being consistent builds trust and authority. It shows that you stick to your word and know what you stand for. You might think that a slip-up of a minor detail, such as when something occurred, won't be noticed and you might be right, but you could also be very wrong.

I know a woman whose story involves a lot of key dates, and she speaks of the timeline of events whenever she tells her story. I noticed that at times her story would waver on when certain events occurred. The overall timeline was correct, but a day or two would be off; and within the story, it was actually a big deal because it all centered on one very big holiday. The other issue was that her story was published online in a number of places, so if they all had discrepancies, then readers and listeners might not trust her or her story. Her story was meant to be one of inspiration, but you can't be inspired by someone you don't trust. The discrepancies can take away from the story and the meaning behind it, and therefore, any goal that was put in place could potentially fail.

Another part of consistency is repetition. You are going to tell the same story over and over again. It might even get old to you, but the truth is that you're speaking to new audiences with every podcast interview, so this is new to them! I think reiterating the same facts and key points in a story is especially important for people who want to become well known. This point reminds me of a recent election campaign I worked on. The candidate I was backing told his life story so many times that I could say it for him and get the facts right. His opponent changed her story every time she spoke. This builds distrust and makes you sound dishonest, so don't be afraid to repeat yourself.

Chances are you don't have me listening to every interview you're doing; therefore, it'll be new information for others!

Another example of how not to tell your story is one from a conference I attended. The speaker was very well known and shared an extremely personal story. It brought the room to tears, and all kinds of emotions were brought up. She definitely told her story in a way that connected her to the participants (great storytelling capabilities!). A couple of months later on social media, she shared her story with the general public . . . and a key detail had been changed. The detail seemed to be changed to appeal to the larger audience and address a current "hot topic," but it also completely changed her story. She had experienced a very traumatic life event that many women go through. Her original story detailed what had happened to her, but her new story turned what she said had happened TO her into a choice SHE had to make. She shared her struggle to make such a decision. Both versions of the story were emotionally difficult and tugged on your heartstrings, BUT to hear one version and then hear another made me question which was true. It put a sour taste in my mouth and had me wondering what other stories she had shared that weren't the full truth or were simply told to appeal to her audience versus being authentic and showing up as the true version of herself.

A good storyteller is someone who tells the truth. Someone who doesn't offer a variety of versions of the story. You can share a collection of stories, but there shouldn't be any discrepancies when it comes to the facts of each one. There are also some personal choices you will need to make when it comes to how detailed you want to be in sharing your story and experiences. Please also keep in mind that depending on what your topic is, some hosts might not always be comfortable in sharing those types of stories. This isn't a reflection on you or your story, but on what the hosts want their show to include. Don't take offense to it; just remember that you aren't going to be right for every podcast, just as every podcast isn't going to be right for you.

Some questions to reflect on:

- Does your story involve other parties?
- Do you need to leave out names or create new ones for certain individuals to protect their privacy?
- Why does this cause or nonprofit speak to you?
- Was there a moment in your life that encouraged you to do more and advocate for this cause?
- Why are you the best candidate for the upcoming election?
- What makes you stand out from the others and makes you not only trustworthy but the best representative for your constituents?
- How did you become THE expert in your field?
- Why are you passionate about what you do?
- What made you write the book you're launching?
- What's your backstory? How did your journey bring you to where you are today, doing what you do?

## ISSUING A TRIGGER WARNING

I want to add an important reminder regarding trigger warnings beforehand. If your story includes trauma or details that could bring up traumatic memories or experiences for others, you should include a trigger warning before sharing your story. A trigger warning is a statement letting the audience know that the material contains content that may be distressing for a certain audience, such as those dealing with grief, those who have suffered from a miscarriage, those who have dealt with suicide, and the like. You can also ask the host to prep the episode with a trigger warning in the introduction of the episode. This is yet another way to ensure you are putting the audience first in what you're doing. I mention speaking to the host about it because not everyone will know that this is something that should be done.

Remember that we all know the reason behind you being interviewed on podcasts is to promote yourself, your business, your platform, your book, and so on. BUT you need to also remember that it is your job to help the listeners with the information you share, the education you offer to them, the inspiration and motivation you provide them. By forgetting to offer a trigger warning, you are putting yourself, your feelings, and your story ahead of the listeners, and that is the opposite of what you should be doing.

# YOUR SPEAKING STRATEGY

## Strategizing on What Anecdotes to Share

Telling your story is one thing, but knowing which parts to include is imperative! We've been creating a strategy this entire time around how you'll pitch yourself and to whom, but you are also going to need a strategy around your talking points. I mentioned earlier that you should be armed with stories for each of your topics. From personal experience, I know you might be wondering what stories you possibly have to share that others will want to hear, so this is going to be an exercise that you will work on over the course of days and weeks and throughout the interviews you do. Much like writing a book, the process of simply starting will create thoughts and ideas in your head. You'll be in the think tank (aka the shower for me!), and suddenly it'll hit you that you have the perfect example or story to go with one of your topics. I have this happen not only during the writing process but when I'm creating content for my social media posts. When these moments happen, write down the thoughts right away. In my shower I have a waterproof notepad and pencils, I have Post-its and a notepad on my desk, and there's always the notes section in your phone. When an idea strikes, write it down! Keep paper and pen next to your bed so that if you wake up to a great idea or it comes to you in a dream, you won't be wondering what it possibly was the next morning.

These stories will eventually all become second nature because you'll create a rhythm for yourself and easily share your stories and examples. The important part of your speaking strategy is to think about what you will share on a topic before it's time to actually do it. Preparation like this will also help alleviate any anxiety before an interview since you'll have a good idea on how you want to approach a subject instead of being in the hot seat at the moment.

Depending on your style, you don't need to write down your story in its entirety. This might help you, depending on the way you operate, so do what works best for you. At a minimum, I recommend you write down a headline for a story or a few sentences to jog your memory. You might even come up with new stories or examples while you're in the middle of an interview, and that's more than OK. What helps me best is an outline of sorts with bullets highlighting parts I don't want to miss. I used this same blueprint when I decided to write this book. I had an overall theme, and I used headlines for chapters and came up with bullet points on what each chapter was to include. This same process can be used for the topics and stories you will be interviewed on. My goal is to get you as prepared as possible going into the interview, which is why I want you to start thinking about this now.

## Tactics for Taming Your Hands While Talking

What kind of a talker are you? Are you animated during a conversation? Do you use your hands a lot while telling a story? Do you tend to play with your hair or a pen during a conversation? Do you tap your feet or shake your leg a bit? If you aren't sure, ask your partner or someone you frequently converse with. Don't take offense at whatever the person's answer is, but do make a note of it and decide if it's something that might be distracting on a podcast interview. If you talk with your hands, then you have the potential to hit the mic and cause a distraction with a loud noise. If you play with your hair and are on video, then it might seem like you don't want to be where you are. If you're clicking away with a pen or accidentally drop it on your desk, you're creating further distraction. Write a list of the conversational habits you have, and place the list on your desk in front of you as a reminder of things you should work on during interviews. Maybe you simply need to slow down. Write yourself a reminder!

## Deciding How to Give Your Freebie to the Audience

You've created an incredible gift for the audience, but how will you introduce it and tie it into the topic and stories you've shared? You'll be asked at the end of every interview how people can find you, and this will be your opportunity to share your website and social media handle and to offer your freebie to the audience as well. This is your call to action that we worked on in Chapter 5! Try to tie it into what you've talked about and how you'd like to offer listeners yet another resource by giving them these tips and tools. Your freebie should somehow be associated with your topic, so bringing the two together should come as second nature.

# MINDSET TOOLS AND TECHNIQUES

I want to take some time to discuss the power of your mindset when it comes to podcast interviews. Whether you realize it or not, if you have a negative mindset, you generally won't land interviews, and those that you do land won't help propel you forward. A positive mindset is going to expand the possibilities that a podcast interview can have for you.

Your mindset is the set of attitudes you hold. In the book *Lead In* by Cathy Burke, she shares four types of mindsets, expanding on the two that most people are familiar with, a growth mindset and a fixed mindset. I won't dive into the additional ones that Cathy discusses, but her book is certainly worth reading if you're interested in learning more about mindsets— in particular, how to enhance yours and how to work with people of a different mindset.

The fixed mindset is limiting. People with a fixed mindset avoid challenges, avoid feedback, feel threatened by others, want to look smart, and give up easily. I think it's interesting that someone with a fixed mindset wants to look smart, because oftentimes that is exactly what someone wants to do by being on a podcast. It's the fact that someone with a fixed mindset either will end up not landing interviews because the person doesn't like hearing no from a host or will be too intimidated by a host with a large show, therefore failing before even starting.

To succeed in podcast guesting, you need to have a growth mindset. This means that you will persevere in the face of failure, have no problem building new skills, find inspiration in the success of others (this is a great time to point out that if the host has been successful, you will be thrilled for the host and say so!), accept criticism, and want to learn and build upon your abilities.

When you are pitching yourself, you will be faced with acceptance as well as rejection, and that's simply part of the process. You can and should learn from the rejections. Figure out if you simply pitched the wrong type of podcast or if your pitch needs some work; either way, a growth mindset will help you in both instances in order to be successful. You might find that at times, pitching yourself is going to be somewhat of a roller coaster. There will be ups and downs, and you'll just be standing in line waiting for the next ride. I've learned that if I can get a grasp on where my headspace is, I can ensure I stay positive no matter what part of the roller coaster ride I'm on, even if I'm waiting in line without a fast pass. I work with my clients on this as well, because my job is to not only pitch and coach them but also support them throughout this entire process. I want to ensure you too have the same support throughout this book and long after. As someone who prefers honesty to silence, I embrace the rejections. It helps you to move on to the next pitch and podcast and allows you to move the card on your Trello board!

Your mindset is made up of your attitude and how you look at a situation. The way you look at it will determine your behavior and how you approach the situation. You'll take action and, the hope is, create a solution based on the action you take. Your actions will produce results, which will enhance your performance, therefore resulting in a positive attitude. One thing leads to another until it comes full circle.

To help illustrate the difference between the two mindsets, I want to show you a side-by-side comparison of the two.

| Fixed Mindset | Growth Mindset |
|---|---|
| Success comes from talent. | Success comes from effort. |
| I'm either smart or dumb. | I can grow my intelligence. |
| I don't like challenges. | I embrace challenges as a chance to grow. |
| Failure means I can't do it. | Failure means I'm learning. |
| Feedback is a personal attack. | Feedback helps me grow. |
| If you succeed, I feel threatened. | If you succeed, I'm inspired. |
| If something's too hard, I give up. | I keep trying even when I'm frustrated. |

There's an obvious positive and negative difference between these two types of mindsets. If you find that you have a fixed mindset, then it will take some internal effort on your part to work toward gaining and maintaining a growth mindset, but rest assured that it can be done. If you believe you can attain a growth mindset, then you've already conquered step one.

It can be a helpful tool to practice positive affirmations and train your brain to get into a growth mindset. You can also write down some of the characteristics I already mentioned of a growth mindset. Recite them to yourself, and put them on a Post-it on your desk for you to look at, and remind yourself daily that you are growing and despite what happens, whether you get a rejection or you trip over your words, you will pick yourself back up and try again.

Getting into the right mindset can also include meditation, journaling, exercise, or simply stretching. Giving yourself the quiet time to reflect on your thoughts and allowing them to lead wherever they might go is a great practice. There are a number of meditations you can download from your phone or listen to on YouTube. One of my favorite people is Sarah Blondin, whose voice and calmness will transport you to feel like you're in another world. Sarah has a podcast and is on Insight Timer, Spotify, the Peloton app, and a plethora of other places. I utilize these techniques outside of podcast interviews as well to help calm my mind during a busy day or to ensure that the start of my day is calm. And if you're like me where this isn't an everyday practice, find a quick 5- or 10-minute guided meditation to start. It doesn't have to be long or time-consuming in order to help. Doing a quick meditation before an interview can also get you into a more relaxed state of mind, especially if it's in the middle of the workday when you're right in the middle of putting out fires or answering emails or it's in between meetings.

## THANKING YOUR HOST

Being a guest in someone's home (a host's podcast is the person's "home") is something you should be grateful for and not take lightly or for granted. A podcast host's home is not only the show but the website and social media accounts as well. I include this so you understand that the podcast host is welcoming you and promoting you on all these platforms that bear the host's name and belong to the host. The host has tied his or her name to yours, and let's be honest, that can be a risky thing at times. Most of us are strangers in the online world, and all we really know about each other is what is out there in the metaverse; yet the host has trusted that you are who you say you are and that you're going to share of yourself freely and impart valuable information to the podcast's audience. This is a really big deal! Part of showing you understand that you get the generosity that's been extended to you is by saying thank you to your host. This is also part of your speaking strategy, because just as you would open a speech by thanking those who welcomed you to the stage, you're to thank your host.

To start, you should thank the host at the end of your interview. That should be a given and the absolute bare minimum for anyone, but this isn't the time to practice minimalism. I want you to go above and beyond a simple thank you. Here's the thing . . . all too often guests offer a verbal thank you and leave it at that. They think that's enough, but it isn't, not by a long shot. In the next chapter, you're going to discover all the ways you can repurpose your interview to turn it into additional marketing content, ways that will also represent a form of thanking your host. Let's start with two basic ways that will put you steps ahead of most guests.

I'll never understand why someone thinks having an interview go live is simply enough, because it just isn't. It's not even close! Immediately following an interview, hop onto Instagram and say thank you to the host by posting something in your Instagram stories. If the interview was video, then I'll ask before or after if the host is OK with me taking a photo of my screen with us together. So far, they've always said yes! I'll post in my Instagram stories saying that I just finished a great interview with the host and tag the host. If the interview didn't have video, then take a selfie with your mic in the shot and tag the host. The host is sharing you with his or her audience, so how beneficial is it for the host to be shared with your audience?! It's something so simple that takes less than two minutes to do and will be greatly appreciated. This is also a great teaser before the interview even airs! I do this not only when I'm being interviewed but when I interview others. I'll be honest with you—I think this is also a really fun way to document these moments for yourself as well. In addition to treasuring autographed books, I love that I have computer screen selfies with people like Eve Rodsky, Kara Goldin, and Zibby Owens.

The majority of podcast hosts create social media assets for their episodes and will ask you for a headshot that they can use for the promotion of the interview. If they don't preemptively send those assets (graphics) to you, then by all means you can and should ask for them. I've noticed a lot of people will post these graphics or share the ones they are tagged in to their Instagram stories, but that's where things end. This is a nice thing to do, BUT an Instagram story stays up for 24 hours and then disappears. Poof, it's gone! Anyone who visits your profile after that day will never know you were interviewed on that show. By all means, put it in your stories, but don't think you're done by a long shot! You also need to add it in your actual Instagram feed via a post and more if you follow my advice.

One of the most ridiculous things I've been told about why someone didn't add the promotional post provided to her in her actual feed was because it didn't match her aesthetic and made the feed look "off-brand." This is where I shake my head and roll my eyes. If the graphic doesn't match your brand and looks "off," then create a new graphic that does match your brand. My clients and I create branded graphics for ourselves on a weekly basis. The entire point is to promote the episode and give the host a shout-out of appreciation to help increase the show's downloads and give you wider recognition for what you're doing. You can create your own graphic templates to ensure your colors and fonts are the same and plug in the cover art, episode title, and episode number of the show you were interviewed on.

Thank your host with more than a 24-hour Instagram story. Create a post that will live in your feed. Tag the host's Instagram account and explain what the episode was about. Encourage your followers to listen to the episode and leave a review if they loved it. These are things that help hosts with their show. More downloads and reviews can equal more exposure for the podcast and more potential advertising dollars if they're looking for sponsors, and it makes the hosts feel really great to see that they're being promoted and appreciated. Make the interview a reciprocal relationship and not just a one-sided one. By reciprocating your appreciation, you'll help the interview grow and ultimately benefit yourself.

## WHAT'S THE HOST UP TO?

The host is producing your interview alone, or possibly with a team. On average, a 30-minute podcast episode takes four hours to produce, and that's leaning toward the conservative side. Once you've recorded your interview, the host will go back and record an intro and an outro. The intro is the part of the episode where the host welcomes the listeners and lets them know what they'll be hearing, offering a bit of information about you that leads up to the actual interview. An outro is the wrap-up of the episode. The host might give some closing thoughts about the interview and thank the listeners for tuning in along with a call to action. There are some hosts that will record the intro with you on the line, but the majority will do this after the fact.

Next comes the editing of the show in which the sound editor listens to the interview and edits out any interruptions, ensures both audio tracks sound similar (i.e., one voice isn't louder than the other), adds the intro and outro, and adds in the music to the beginning and end of the show; and if there are sponsors, the editor adds in any audio around that.

The complete audio file can then be transcribed using a service such as Otter.ai or Descript. When a podcast host transcribes a show and posts it with show notes on the host's website, it ensures the show is accessible for an audience outside of the hearing community. From a transcription, a host can also then scan the conversation for quotes to use and turn into graphics for various social media platforms.

Most podcasts will also create show notes for each episode. Show notes can be long- or short-form blog posts that are posted to podcast platforms and the host's website. They offer a summary of the episode, main talking points, and links that are mentioned in the episode, along with how to reach the guest. Hosts will utilize show notes to expand the search of their show. Remember that since a podcast is a listening form of content, a host needs to have something such as show notes in order to make the show searchable on platforms like Google. By ensuring there are show notes on a website and that they are SEO friendly, a show can garner a much greater reach than only having it on podcast listening platforms.

Once the episode is edited and transcribed and the show notes are written, graphics will be created. Graphics are created in a variety of sizes to fit each social media platform. Many use the guest's headshot (yours!) as part of the graphic, and quotes from the guest might be used as another graphic. When all these steps have been completed, the audio file will then be uploaded to the podcast's host (this term of "host" refers to the platform that distributes the really simple syndication, or RSS, feed to other podcast listening platforms). The host can be thought of as the heart, and the RSS feed is the veins carrying blood to the rest of the body, or all the listening devices. The episode graphic can also be uploaded to this platform and scheduled in advance. The host will then add the show notes and graphics and embed the podcast player link to the podcast's website, schedule social media posts for the episode, and let the guest know when the interview has gone live. Now you can fully understand why 30 minutes of a conversation turns into four hours of actual work!

## EXERCISE

### Mastering Your Stories and Creating a Positive Mindset

#### Storytelling

You've already created your expert speaking topics, and now it's time to ensure you have stories that you can weave throughout your interview that not only share more about who you are and what your journey is like but that will also inspire listeners. Oftentimes we hear people sharing their "why" . . . why do they pursue the passions, hobbies, careers, missions that they do? The reasoning behind why you do what you do should be included in your story. You don't need to use the exact wording of "This is why I do what I do," but it should be evident in what you share with the audience.

Take some time to write down the answers to the questions I presented earlier in the chapter:

- Does your story involve other parties?

- Do you need to leave out names or create new ones for certain individuals to protect their privacy?
- Why does this cause or nonprofit speak to you?
- Was there a moment in your life that encouraged you to do more and advocate for this cause?
- Why are you the best candidate for the upcoming election?
- What makes you stand out from the others and makes you not only trustworthy but the best representative for your constituents?
- How did you become THE expert in your field?
- Why are you passionate about what you do?
- What made you write the book you're launching?
- What's your backstory? How did your journey bring you to where you are today, doing what you do?

As you retell your story over and over, you'll find a flow with what you share, and your memory might be jogged by other moments or stories that are applicable. Know that this will be a work in progress when you start out and then you'll hit your stride!

### Researching Your Host

If you've already booked an interview, then take some time to research your host and the show a bit further. Listen to another episode or two. Find out if the host has a certain line of questioning he or she uses. Is there one question the host asks every single guest? Consider your answer before the interview. You don't have to write it down and read the answer, but it's always helpful to know what's coming so you aren't taken by surprise and so the host knows you've done your homework. Check out your host's social media pages, and read the About page on the host's website. If there's something that really sticks out at you, make a note of it so you can bring it into the conversation if appropriate. When a guest does this with me, I feel a more genuine connection happening because I'm grateful to know that the guest was excited enough about our interview to plan ahead.

### Mindset Work

What does your current mindset look like? Are there roadblocks telling you that maybe you aren't the right person to be interviewed? Is impostor syndrome rearing its ugly head? Let's get rid of the negativity now! Write out the negatives, and right next to them, write out your counterargument. Recite the counterarguments out loud. *Reminder:* You've worked hard to get where you are. You are the expert in your field. Your story and message matter. You have the power to change someone's life by sharing your knowledge and story. You owe it to yourself and to the world to share your voice.

For example:

- **Negative.** My story isn't as important as someone else's.
- **Counterargument.** My story is unique and has the power to change someone's life. No one in the world can tell my story the way I can, nor has anyone experienced what I have.

Practice saying the affirmations in this chapter for a growth mindset. What you tell yourself is what you will believe.

## SUMMARY

Knowing your story and telling it as truthfully and as vulnerably as you can is what is going to make you a great storyteller and a sought-after podcast guest. Be yourself. Believe in yourself. This is what authenticity truly is, and you have the power and the gifts to make this happen. Go the extra mile and do your homework on the person who will be interviewing you. A podcast interview is a give-and-take. Throughout this process, remember that although this is about you, it's not really about you!

# YOUR NAME IN LIGHTS

## MAXIMIZING YOUR PODCAST INTERVIEWS BY REPURPOSING THEM INTO MORE MARKETING CONTENT

You've recorded the interview and posted a story on Instagram, so now what? The biggest mistake I see podcast guests make is thinking that they're done at this point. That couldn't be further from the truth. You are reading this book and wanting to be a podcast guest to increase your visibility, and that takes going the extra mile. It takes more than just the 30-minute interview you recorded to make an impact and impression, as well as to make it worth your while to even be recording these interviews.

We all want the best bang for our buck when it comes to most things in life. The podcast interview you recorded was free to you, and now I'm going to share how you can gain a ridiculous amount of mileage out of those 30 minutes and create content that is going to have your marketing team high-fiving you. (I am my marketing team, so you can jump for joy along with me if you are your team!)

Repurposing content is the ability to take one piece of content (your podcast interview) and turn it into multiple pieces of content that can be used across different platforms. Repurposing content is like the saying "Killing two birds with one stone." You're going to spend 30 minutes on an interview and walk away with multiple pieces of content for every social media account you have, your website, and more. Repurposing your content is going to make you appear in more places and elevate your visibility to the world.

If repurposing is so great, why isn't everyone doing it? Because it can take some time up front and people don't understand the value in repurposing content. I'm sure you've heard people complain about how much time it takes to create social media posts (hey, I can raise my hand on this one), but you can create more than a week's worth of content with a single podcast episode, so why not do it?! It doesn't need to take as much time as some think . . . you just need to create a process and graphic templates; then it's plug-and-play. Because we are now friends, I'm going to make sure you have everything you need to make this happen and to make it easy! This is also something you could easily outsource if you wanted to. I like to point out the areas where you can enlist the help of others because you don't need to do this alone, and there are ways to find help that isn't going to cost you an arm and a leg while saving you valuable time . . . time to make more money!

We are going to go over how you can repurpose your interviews for various platforms and how to promote them. I get that you might not feel comfortable promoting yourself, because a lot of my clients say this. It can feel a bit weird and awkward to post quotes of yourself, but that's exactly how you become known as a thought leader in your space. Learn to embrace it. Why promote the content of someone else when yours is worth promoting and sharing? We'll approach that roadblock at full speed, and I'll show you how to breach that barrier! You might feel like you're repeating yourself by posting the same content in various places. Trust me when I say you are NOT repeating yourself. With varying algorithms and followers that are specific to certain platforms, the chances of your followers seeing your content in every location at the same time is extremely rare! In fact, oftentimes you can post the same content to the same platform, and it'll be seen by different followers. You will feel like you've been harping on the same topic or interview, but your followers certainly will not. In addition to all of this, followers aren't going to remember what you posted two months ago, let alone a year ago!

## THE AFTER-PARTY

I can't remember when I first heard the term "after-party," but I do remember days when that was a question that would come up—"Where's the after-party at?" It was probably in college! Because for some reason the preparty and actual party just simply aren't enough for one evening! What about when there isn't a true after-party and everyone heads home? What comes after that? From my experience as a 40-something-year-old, it's usually talk of when the next get-together will be. For those a decade or two younger than me, it might include making future plans and some posting on social media about what a great time everybody had and photos featuring the food, the cocktails that were mixed or the wine that was tasted, and people smiling and laughing—showing what a great time looks like.

Just because the evening came to a close doesn't mean that the sharing of the memories is over. Heck, you might even be reminiscing the next week or month about what a great time it was to get together with friends and post something about it. I see and receive messages from friends when memories pop up from a year (or even five years!) ago recalling what fun we had. Let's also not forget that for almost two years, we weren't able to have dinner parties or happy hours or get together in a confined space, so getting to relive the parties of the past and post-pandemic present is something we are seeing more of because we didn't realize what we had until it was gone. Just because the party ends and everyone goes home doesn't mean that the memories don't live on and stop being shared. The same goes for a podcast interview. The recording may be over, but the message doesn't stop being shared.

---

## GETTING THE MOST OUT OF YOUR PODCAST INTERVIEWS— REPURPOSING THEM

I think it's worth repeating because I believe so strongly in this . . . just because you've finished recording the interview does not mean that you're all done with the interview. The interview itself is extremely important, but the content that you create from the interview is where you are going to see the most benefit. If you do your best to repurpose content, you're going to increase the visibility of that interview exponentially. Repurposing content simply means that you are taking a piece of big content, a podcast interview in this case, and turning it into bite-size pieces of content for other platforms, such as your social media accounts.

A common goal among business owners, senior executives, and others is to be seen as a thought leader. A thought leader means being the true authority in your field and someone who generates and shares high-quality content. You want to be the go-to person for whatever it is you do and know. We've already discussed the importance of being generous with your knowledge in the interview, and now we are going to take that generosity and further distribute it across multiple channels and platforms to increase your visibility and that of your business, cause, and mission. Creating content is one of the most time-consuming tasks that anyone with a social media presence has. It takes time to know what to say and to create graphics to fit the content, schedule your posts, utilize the right hashtags, and so on. This is a part that sounds daunting, but since this book is about making things simple . . . I'm going to do just that for you!

The key to repurposing content is to make it as easy and plug-and-play as possible. I get that you don't have a ton of extra time on your hands because I'm in the same boat, but I also know that you are already creating daily and weekly content . . . posting on Instagram, adding to your stories, tweeting out your thoughts and tips, posting on LinkedIn about best practices, sharing on Facebook the importance of what you do, and much more. Some people create different posts for each of these platforms; yet the only thing you really need to do is create a different-sized graphic, change the caption to fit the space, and know whether or not hashtags should be included in the caption based on the platform. With all the algorithms changing on a daily basis, you can absolutely post the same content on all the platforms because chances are that not all your followers have seen it—therefore, they won't be seeing it multiple times. Sorry to sound like a Debbie Downer, but that's the truth and all the more reason why you should make it a priority to post in multiple places in order to reach the maximum amount of people and another reason why you shouldn't be spending a ton of time creating different content for every single platform on a daily basis. You can even use a free scheduling tool to post it (I use Later). I want to make all of this as easy and accessible for you as possible. If it's not simple, then find a way to simplify it!

Here are some of the ways you can repurpose your interviews that I'll be discussing more in depth:

- Adding a blog post on your website with graphics and an embedded player to hear the episode
- Using the same blog post on Medium
- Creating quote graphics for Instagram, Threads, LinkedIn, X, Facebook, and Pinterest
- Creating episode graphics that fit your brand for Instagram, Threads, LinkedIn, X, Facebook, and Pinterest
- Using the content for your email list
- Creating audiograms (a still graphic with audio attached) with captions for Instagram Stories, Pinterest, Facebook, and TikTok

# TRANSCRIPTS

A lot of podcasters work hard to make their show accessible to all audiences by providing a transcript of their episodes right on their website. Remember that a podcast is normally for the hearing community, but when you add a transcript, it becomes accessible for the deaf community; and if you add video with captions, it becomes accessible to everyone. If you see that the host does this, please save yourself an extra step and download the transcript file from the host's website. Utilizing a transcript can be a great way to easily find quotes of yourself to create content for your platforms. If you take my advice (which you should!), you'll also add the transcript to your blog post on your own website, along with embedding a podcast player link (more on that below). I'm a big advocate for accessibility and inclusion; therefore, you should always offer a transcript.

If a transcript is not made available, you can download the audio file from the host's website or RSS feed (the website the host uses to submit his or her website to all podcast platforms such as Libsyn, Podbean, etc.). Take the audio file and upload it to Otter.ai or Descript—both are free platforms that will turn your audio into a transcript. The transcript can then be edited and downloaded as a PDF or other file format and uploaded to your website.

# QUICK TIP: EMBED
# A PODCAST PLAYER LINK

This is a tip that I'm hoping catches on for more podcast guests because this is something most hosts and guests don't think about. You can easily embed a link to the podcast on your website so that visitors don't even need to leave your page to listen! Ask the host for the embed code to put it on your website. A host will love this because it provides the host with more downloads of the episode! The code is an HTML link that you can easily add to your blog post. This ensures that your website visitors not only can listen to your interview but don't have to leave your site to hear it.

Don't worry if you aren't a tech-savvy person. You don't need to know about coding to make this work. Depending on what platform you use for your website, there should be a box in which the code can be entered. I utilize Elementor for my WordPress website, and for me, it's called a "short code." For Squarespace websites, you will add a block and select "Embed" as the type. It's going to be as simple as copy and paste and literally the only time I'll advocate for copy and paste!

## GRAPHIC TEMPLATES

Most of the time, but not all, the host will send you social media assets or graphics for you to promote your interview. I highly suggest using them, but if you (or your marketing team) are a stickler for staying "on brand" with the fonts and colors you use, then you can create graphic templates and use them. I do this for myself and for my agency to showcase where my clients have been featured each week. My graphics match my branding in color and font, and they include my clients' headshots and the podcasts they were interviewed on . . . once again killing two birds with one stone! I save the podcast cover art from Google to represent the podcast.

I love using Canva because it has a free option, but feel free to use any graphic program that you're comfortable with. The goal is to create templates that you can utilize and are easy! You're going to need to create two different sizes for templates to use on the various platforms. One will be a square (Instagram feed, Facebook, LinkedIn), and the other will be a rectangle (Instagram stories, Pinterest). There are a ton of templates to choose from within Canva, or you can create your own. For the templates in Canva, you can swap out the stock photos it uses, change the font and colors, and add your logo. This is where you have creative freedom!

There will be certain information that should go on every template; therefore, you can create text boxes for this information. The content that you will want to ensure goes on to each template includes:

- Podcast name
- Episode title
- Episode number

You should create graphic templates for the episode itself, along with templates that allow you to insert a quote. Figures 7.1 and 7.2 illustrate how I repurpose my own interviews on other shows. Oftentimes a podcast will provide you with quotes that it uses, but in my experience, the majority will not. This is why downloading a transcript is a great idea and an easy way to identify great quotes for yourself.

**FIGURE 7.1**    Instagram graphic for my interview on *The Purpose Show*

As much as I love being here, this episode is not about me. This is about the content and the knowledge that I get to share with your audience and what they can gain from it.

Listeners To Leads
Episode 2

**FIGURE 7.2**  Instagram graphic utilizing a quote from a podcast interivew

You can create these templates from scratch or use the ones I've created for you. Simply go to the websites below and select "use template for a new design" in Canva.

- **Facebook templates,** https://bit.ly/FBPod Templates
- **Pinterest templates,** https://bit.ly/PinterestPodTemplates
- **IG story templates,** https://bit.ly/IGStoryPodTemplates
- **IG feed templates,** https://bit.ly/IGPodTemplates

## BLOG POSTS AND YOUR WEBSITE

The majority of podcasters write and post show notes to their website. Show notes are a written synopsis or overview of what the episode is about. They vary in formats, but essentially are a blog post that helps a website's SEO and are simply another way of increasing the visibility of a podcast. The most common show note formats include a summary of the entire episode, some topic headlines that are SEO friendly, a call to action, and links that were mentioned in the episode. You can copy and paste the show notes from the podcast you were interviewed on. I highly recommend that you create a version of show notes (whether you create your own or use the ones from the host) for your website for every podcast appearance you make. Below I'm providing you with an outline and example of show notes that you can use for yourself. Include a link to the transcript to help your website audience as well, and don't forget to embed your podcast player link. I post mine at the top of the blog post so that the show can be listened to right away. Be sure to also include at least one graphic that you created in a rectangular form because you'll be able to utilize this on Pinterest (two birds, one stone!).

## Blog Post—Show Notes Template

Your show notes template for your blog post should include:

- Episode title, title of podcast and link, episode number
- Summary of the episode
- Topics that were highlighted
- Summary of each topic
- Call to action
- Links mentioned in the episode (These are links to websites, podcast episodes, books, or anything else in the episode so that you can direct listeners to the site.)

## Show Notes Sample

The following will give you a good idea of what your show notes should look like.

## EXAMPLE

### Show Notes: The Mindfulness Challenge

Have you ever considered how your mindset might be affecting your entire life? As a word and a concept, "mindset" is a relatively new one for me, but once I started to work on having a positive mindset in my business, I quickly realized that it's setting out a positive intention into the world, and it actually works. This week I launched a Mindfulness Challenge in which we are resetting our mindsets and creating a new routine that involves meditation, movement, food, and more. Now is one of the best times to start working on becoming more mindful of what your actions are doing to affect your life and to create habits that will ensure you are making positive changes. I for one need this challenge more than ever and am so excited to be doing it alongside so many of you!

Are you ready to become more mindful? Here's what we're going to talk about:

- What does "mindset" mean?
- Recognizing your priorities in life
- The Mindfulness Challenge

Now, let's examine each one of these items in more detail.

## What Does Mindset Mean?

The word "mindset" is one that I wasn't familiar with in the corporate world. When I became an entrepreneur, this word popped up everywhere. I didn't start to believe in it or actually practice it until I lost my first client. I decided that instead of worrying and being upset over it, I would practice positive thinking and make sure my mindset was positive. I told myself a bigger client who was a better fit would replace the one I lost, and it happened almost instantly. I became a believer in working on my mindset and in the difference it can make in life.

### Recognizing Your Priorities in Life

As I worked on this episode and the Mindfulness Challenge, my kids interrupted me. And they didn't do it in a small way . . . they cranked up Justin Timberlake on the TV and demanded a dance party—because no one can stop the feeling! I stopped what I was doing and danced like a crazy person. We sang at the top of our lungs and laughed and had the best time ever. THIS is what my priority in life needs to be, and this is what I hope to do more of with this Mindfulness Challenge. I want to better recognize my priorities and to ensure that I honor them in everything I do.

### The Mindfulness Challenge

The Mindfulness Challenge has kicked off, but you can still join us! We are working on a new exercise every day that ranges from meditation to cooking to exercise to gratitude and more. By working on one thing every day, we are going to create a new routine in which we practice these things more often. We want to build a routine in which we are grateful for what we have and show our bodies and minds that we are grateful for them as well. It might sound full of woo-woo, but I promise you it isn't!

Who is ready for a mindset reset? Join the challenge!

**Links Mentioned** (Note that I always leave links as plural in my template—there might only be one link mentioned, but the header is always the same in my posts.)

Your Simplified Podcast Launch Course, www.themlgcollective/podcastcourse.

# AUDIOGRAMS

Audiograms are used by a lot of podcasters as a teaser for their episodes. An audiogram has a static image (one of the graphics created for the episode), and a software program adds the audio file to the graphic. You have the ability to select the time stamp (an audio clip, normally under one minute based on the social media platform you're using) you want to use and add a waveform, which consists of lines or dots in different colors and even includes captions. Two great programs you can use to create your own audiograms are Wavve and Headliner. Both programs have free and low-cost options to choose from.

Audiograms are great for Instagram stories and Pinterest. Ideally, your clip should be 60 seconds or less because that's what Instagram stories allow. The clip will be broken down into 15-second segments within the Instagram platform automatically.

The reason behind creating audiograms is that they are like a preview of a movie. You can take a great portion of the interview and let people hear it as a hook to reel them in to go listen to the rest of the episode. They're small soundbites of what the rest of the interview includes.

## SOCIAL MEDIA PLATFORMS—WHAT YOU NEED FOR EACH ONE

These days there are a number of social media platforms, and honestly, they seem to keep growing (Hey Clubhouse! Hey Mastodon! Hey Post!). You need to figure out which platforms are best for you. Which ones are your listeners using, and which ones align with your purpose? As I mentioned in the introduction, please don't feel you need to be on all of them or even post every way possible on each of them. Personally, I have no interest in creating short videos and putting them on Instagram reels or TikTok, so at the time of writing this, I don't. That might change in the future, but for now I don't see it as a valuable use of my time. I will say that the more places you can be, then obviously the more people you can reach, so if you post on all these platforms, good for you. Don't feel pressure to do so though. Try one or two if you aren't already using them.

On the off chance that you aren't using some of these social media platforms, then I want to give you some tips on how to post and utilize them to the best of your ability. There is always more you can do, but these are the basics.

## Instagram

Instagram has a post (these are your posts that show up when someone visits your profile or when someone opens the app and scrolls the feed), stories (posts that disappear after 24 hours), reels (videos that you can post to your feed and share in your stories), and a live option that can also be turned into a post. You can utilize all these functions to promote your podcast interviews:

- **Creating a post.** Use a square graphic and write a mini blog post of what the episode is about. Tag (use @ and the podcast host's username) the host or podcast and give followers a call to action, whether it's to listen to the episode, visit your website for the show notes, download a freebie, share something about themselves or the episode that they enjoyed, and so on. Add hashtags (up to 30) that are relevant to you and the episode (search the hashtags before using them to make sure they've been used less than 1 million times). Please note that just because you can use a certain number of hashtags on Instagram doesn't mean you should post the max amount!

- **Creating a story.** Use a rectangular-sized graphic. You can link to the episode or your show notes, tag the host or podcast, and add hashtags (up to 10). You can also use an audiogram in your stories. You can add your stories to your highlights, which will ensure the story stays up for longer than 24 hours. You can create a highlight just for your podcast interviews and save up to 100 stories for each highlight.

- **Creating a reel.** Any videos posted to Instagram are turned into a reel; therefore, if you want to create a video about the episode or have a video clip from the interview, you can post this as a reel and add a caption.

- **Going live.** The Instagram algorithm loves when you use all the features and functionality of the app, so if you feel comfortable and want to go live, go for it! You can jump on and say hello to your followers and tell them to go listen to your latest interview and share what it was about. It's a great way to connect with your audience.

- **Adding to your profile.** There's an option for you to have your website in your profile. Instead of having just your website, I would advise you to create a link with a menu of links. I utilize Elementor for my WordPress website, and it has menu options, so I've created a "social" one where I can post links to recent interviews, my freebies, my website, the podcast, and so on. You can also utilize Linktree for free to create one link that showcases all your links for followers.

- **Threads.** With the addition of Threads to Instagram, you can utilize the tweet you're creating for X and also include the clickable link to your interview. At the time of writing this book, hashtags still weren't a function in Threads, so no need to add those.

## Facebook

Facebook has a post option and a story option. I'm more keen on utilizing just the post function. If you have a business page, you can post your interviews to that and/or your personal Facebook page.

- **Creating a post.** You can use the square image of the episode or quotes for your graphic. Include a synopsis of the interview, a link to the interview, and a call to action.

## LinkedIn

LinkedIn is a great platform for professional networking and for showcasing yourself as a thought leader and expert.

- **Creating a post.** Use the square image of the episode or quote for your graphic and include a synopsis of the interview, a link to listen, and a call to action. The great thing about LinkedIn is that when someone likes your post, it shows up in the feeds of everyone that is connected with that person, therefore creating more exposure for you.

## X (Formerly Known as Twitter)

X is all too often forgotten by many these days and truly shouldn't be. Trust me when I tell you that all the journalists are hanging out on X and I get the most up-to-date information from my X feed. X is short and sweet and offers a wealth of information. While I was writing this book, Twitter was purchased by Elon Musk and has gone through some interesting twists and turns. I recently created a Post account in case X implodes, but until then, I will continue to advocate using X as a great platform to connect and network with people in your industry and journalists.

- **Creating a tweet.** You can only use 280 characters in a tweet, so you are going to want to get right to the point! Mention what your topic is and tag the host. You can also link to the episode or show notes and add a graphic. X allows for hashtags, and I would recommend using two as a best practice. To also save space, shorten the link by creating a bit.ly link for your interview.

## Pinterest

Gone are the days of Pinterest being a platform for just DIY crafts, home decor, and recipes. More and more users are looking for content that pertains to their work, marketing, and expert topics.

- **Creating a pin.** Use a rectangular-sized graphic for your pin (if you've used one on your website, you can pin directly from the website). Use keywords in your pin description, and create a call to action. You can also add hashtags that are searchable, although this isn't a highly utilized function of the platform.
- **Creating a board.** Create a board for all your podcast interviews so that you can pin your interviews all in one place.

## MEDIUM—REPURPOSE YOUR BLOG POST

Medium.com is an online publishing platform that you can post to. In other words, it's like having a blog website that you don't have to manage, just post to. You can create articles by simply pasting a link to your show notes, OR you can write a new blog post about your interview. This is simply another great way to gain exposure and get more hits on Google.

## EMAIL LIST

You should already have an email list that continues to grow with your podcast interviews. If you're emailing your list weekly or biweekly, you can either add an entire newsletter about every podcast interview or simply insert a link and let your readers know that you were recently featured on a podcast and ask them to head over and listen to it.

The overall goal in all of this is to reach as many of your followers as possible. We know that not everyone is going to see your post or open up your email; therefore, you need to be placing your content in as many places as possible in the hope that it will be seen.

## OVERCOMING THE BARRIERS OF SELF-PROMOTION

Self-promotion is the action of promoting or publicizing oneself or one's activities. Right now, you might be worried that sharing your podcast interviews is a form of self-promotion and you're simply not comfortable with it. I absolutely get that, and it's a concern that comes up for my clients quite often and is something I've also had to overcome. I've worked with clients before, during, and after the pandemic; during the insurrection on January 6; through the reversal of *Roe v. Wade*; and during every other event that America has experienced since 2018. Here's the thing about everything we, as Americans, have been living through: It's been nonstop. Just when you think things couldn't get worse or another major event couldn't possibly happen, someone says, "Hold my beer!"

Events in the news and our government have been extremely heavy, and I have had clients who said they don't feel like they can or should share their interviews because it detracts from what is going on in the world. I disagree. You need to share your interviews. If you are doing podcast interviews the way this book instructs you to and are sharing your experience, expertise, and message and going out of your way to help other people, then it's your duty to let others know they can hear more from you. Sharing these interviews that include your story is a way to help someone else who might just be waiting to hear from you to know they aren't alone. I'd go as far as saying it's your responsibility to ensure your message is reaching as many people as possible because every story has the power to change the life of at least one person. Your story is powerful! You're also helping out another human being—the host—by promoting the host's podcast. We are all still working during the good and bad times; therefore, these bad times are when a lot of us need the most help when it comes to promoting our work or podcasts.

I had this very conversation with Elizabeth, my client who is mentioned earlier in the book. She had wrapped up three incredible interviews recounting her job burnout experience and how she overcame it—and what she was doing to ensure she never burned out in the future. The interviews went live the same week that *Roe v. Wade* was overturned, there were more mass shootings in our country, and much more. Elizabeth came to me and said she was uncomfortable and didn't know how to share these interviews because she felt it was self-promoting during a time when the focus shouldn't be on her. My conversation with Elizabeth went like this: Through the years of the pandemic and before, people were experiencing burnout. Today, more and more are feeling burned out, not only at work but in life overall (see the list of events above!). We are going through the most turbulent times, and what I personally feel we all need is to hear stories of resilience, stories that tell us burnout can happen but there are ways that we can avoid it or get through it. Elizabeth's story is about all of that and more. She owes it to the rest of us to share her story of resilience and to help those who are worried about burning out at work or at home. We need to know we aren't alone and we will get through this.

It was a light-bulb moment. Elizabeth went on to share her interviews and received hundreds of likes and garnered support from followers and strangers. They thanked her for sharing her story because it was needed.

I promise you that someone listening has been waiting to hear from you. If you don't share your interviews, then how will the person hear it? This isn't about you. This is about the audience. Share your interviews not to elevate yourself but to help those who need to hear your story, join your mission, have hope for the future, know they can overcome whatever it is they're going through, be inspired, and more.

## MEASURING THE ROI OF YOUR INTERVIEWS

People like to know what the return on their investment is. I'm particular in knowing the facts when it comes to money, but it's just as important when it comes to your podcast interviews. How can you figure out the ROI of the time you're spending on podcast interviews? Since I like to be as candid as possible, I'm going to tell you that it can be difficult to pinpoint certain numbers. The number of downloads isn't readily available for podcasts and not something that is normally requested from hosts . . . it's just not commonplace, but there's no reason you couldn't ask. I will tell you though that the problem will lie in when you should ask for download numbers since they will be constantly changing. In addition to the numbers changing, they aren't really telling you if you've gotten a return on the interview.

When you give out your freebie or have your call to action, you should create a unique bit.ly link for each podcast you interview on. This will be a direct way for you to see how many people downloaded your content after listening to your interview on a show and is a great way to measure what you gained from a particular show.

Another way to measure your podcast interview ROI is to pay attention to where your new clients are coming from. I have a form on my website for people who would like to work with me, and I specifically ask how they heard about me. If it's from a podcast interview, then I know that there was value and a return on that particular show. Other types of returns can come in the form of being asked to be on other shows or to speak at a conference. I've had clients who end up getting new jobs because of appearing on a podcast; and sometimes as a result of being on the show, hosts ask to work with them, they've been asked to contribute to a book, they've been asked to be interviewed for a magazine feature, they've created partnerships and collaborations on future projects, they've gotten more book sales, and much more.

The ROI on your podcast interviews will come down to what you're looking to get out of them. It will also come down to where you direct listeners to go after hearing your interview and what your call to action has been for them. You get to be in charge of the return you're looking for, so don't squander this opportunity!

## WHAT'S THE HOST UP TO?

The host is doing exactly what you are . . . creating graphic templates to use for every episode. Podcast hosts want to ensure their downloads increase along with their audience reach; therefore, it's important that they share their episodes in as many places as possible. It's simply not enough to post an episode and hope for the best. I created a podcast repurposing course that identifies a minimum of 14 different ways a host can repurpose a single episode. It's imperative to consistently show up with your episodes as a host (and a guest!) and share the episodes often. A host will air older episodes for several reasons: to refresh the memories of those who heard the episodes a while ago, to share them with those who might have missed them the first time around, and to share them with listeners who only recently started listening to their show. Remember that you might sound repetitive to yourself, but it is fresh content for followers!

---

## EXERCISE

### Create Graphic Templates

You are going to create four graphic templates in Canva or another graphic design software program of your choice:

- Square interview announcement template
- Rectangle interview announcement template
- Square quote template
- Rectangle quote template

Make sure you include areas for your headshot, the podcast cover art, the podcast show name, the episode title, and the episode number. Utilize your own branding colors and fonts, and add your logo in if you have one.

## SUMMARY

I want you to get the most out of your podcast interviews, and sharing them is the way to do it. Repurposing your interviews creates incredible marketing content that can be spread across multiple platforms and allows you to have content that doesn't need to be created from scratch. It is going to save you time while appearing to have taken up a lot of time. Go into this process with a want to help others, and it won't feel like self-promotion. Do the work up front by creating templates so that you will save time for yourself in the long run. Repurposing your content is going to increase your visibility and elevate how you are seen as a thought leader.

# YOUR HIGHLIGHT REEL

## CREATING A MEDIA/PRESS PAGE
## WITH ALL YOUR INTERVIEWS

Your website should be up and running before you start doing podcast interviews. The goal of a website is to establish your online presence and have a place to direct people. Your website should already encompass who you are—it should explain what your business, platform, or book is about; house your freebies; inform visitors on how to contact you and follow you; AND showcase all the places you've been featured and interviewed.

Your media page, or press page (the terms can be interchangeable, and I am not going play favorites—I'm calling it a "media/press page"!), is a place where anyone can go to see updates on you and/or your company and where the media has interviewed or featured you, and it can also be where you keep press releases that have gone live. Essentially it's all the media that is about you in one place! Your media/press page is where the press, journalists, and podcast hosts will go to see who else has featured you and find other relevant information about you. It's also a place for you to house pertinent information for the press and podcasts to gather without having to contact you directly. This page is going to be a one-stop shop for hosts who want to interview you in the future to not only see where you've already been, but gather all the additional resources they'll need for when it's time to interview you without having to ask you for it.

A media/press page allows for evergreen promotion because it's never going to change that you received the features, awards, and interviews that you did. Those will remain in perpetuity (such a great legal word!); therefore, it is evergreen content that can continue to be promoted.

A press page includes:

- Your bio and a description of your company, platform, or book
- Your headshots that are approved for download
- Press and podcast mentions and interviews (with links!)
- Awards you've received
- Media kit
- Press contact information
- Logo files that can be downloaded (if you have a book, the cover art should also be included)

Depending on what you do, such as whether you're an entrepreneur, politician, advocate, activist, or rising thought leader, you might also include elections you've won, presentations or talks you've completed (e.g., TED Talks), bills or policies you've gotten passed, and the like.

## THE NEXT INVITATION

You had a blast at the last Netflix-and-chill night, or no champagne—no gain night, or rustic BBQ or charcuterie night, and you met some great new friends. This was how my friend Cindy and I met. We hit it off at a dinner party that our mutual friend Sara hosted. This was back when the app "Bump" was a thing (this was an app where if you both had it on your phone, opened it, and bumped phones, your contact information would be exchanged), and we "bumped" each other at the dinner table. The next time Cindy was hosting a happy hour at her house, I received an invitation thanks to having already met and having such a fun conversation. Cindy and I have now been friends for over 10 years and still get together every month!

Podcast hosts are going to head to your media page and see where you've been. They might listen to an interview or two, and based on that one-sided interaction, they might invite you to be a guest on their show. A positive referral is made when you've been invited to be a guest on a show, just as one is made by a friend who invites you to meet more of his or her friends. You've already passed the hot seat questions!

---

# CREATING YOUR MEDIA/PRESS PAGE

## Your Previous Interviews and Features

Remember back in Chapter 2 when we gathered all the interviews you'd already done and all the places where you'd been mentioned? These are going to come in handy once again! If you work with a website designer or developer, you'll be giving the person all this information as well. For the podcasts and outlets you were interviewed for, you can download the cover art for the podcasts and logos for any news outlets, OR you can utilize an icon that designates if you did a podcast interview, such as a microphone (🎤), a newspaper (📰), or a television (🖥). The style is completely up to you because it should best represent the look and feel of your brand. I would encourage you to look at the media/press pages of other people in AND out of your space to get a feel for what you like. There might be a layout that catches your eye or certain icons that speak to you. Use that inspiration for your page. This is by no means copying, because you aren't taking other people's material or utilizing their interviews. We are just looking at layouts, templates, and the like.

In addition to having either the cover art or icons/emojis selected for your interviews, you'll also need to match each interview up with the live link. This will allow visitors to simply click on the cover art or icon and be redirected to your interview. Since the podcast name is on the cover art, you can choose whether to include that or not, but I would highly suggest you add the title of your episode under the cover art or icon. If you're not using the cover art of the podcast, you should definitely include the name of the podcast show in addition to the episode title.

## Your Bio—the Long and the Short of It

You should offer two bios on your media/press page, a short and concise one of about three to five sentences and a longer one that is more all-encompassing. Oftentimes a host will want to read your full bio to get a feel for who you are, what you've done, and what you're about. While this is great information, it can be too long to read during a podcast intro; therefore, the concise bio is best used for that. The same goes for journalists who might use a quote from you. It's much easier to simply add a sentence or a few descriptive words about you, rather than take up an entire paragraph or two with your background. Remember that in journalism, words are prime real estate!

## Smile for the Camera—Approved Headshots

Go through your headshots and select your favorites, up to five. Upload them to your media/press page beneath the following note: "The headshots below are approved for use. Please give credit to the photographer [*insert photographer's name*]."

You might be wondering why you'd offer your headshots to be readily available for download from your website. For starters, this ensures that the photos you want to use to promote yourself are easily accessible. Don't ever forget that many people utilize Google as a resource for images, not just for information, and you'd be surprised at what images might pop up when your name is googled. Have you tried it? Take a pause from reading right now, google your name, and click on "Images" to see what comes up.

Were you surprised by what you saw? Were there specific photos that you'd prefer a host or journalist doesn't use? By offering your headshots on your website for download, you are controlling what is approved by you and what people use. You are also ensuring that your photographer receives the proper photo credit deserved, along with the appreciated backlink potentials (when someone links back to your website to help drive more traffic)!

In addition to including interviews and features, your media/press page is a great place to also mention your other various accolades, such as awards and rankings.

## YOUR DOWNLOADABLE MEDIA KIT

You've created a beautiful media kit that has all your pertinent information that will hook a podcast host in, so why not share it on your media/press page? This is another great option for hosts to download your bio and see everything there is about you. Don't forget that it's filled with hyperlinks, which make it easy for people to download and continue clicking away!

I recommend you include a PDF version that hosts can download since this ensures the links are there and it mimics what you would include in your pitch.

## BOOKING CONTACT INFORMATION

You've hooked and reeled a host in. The host wants to book you. The host can download all your marketing materials, but how does the host contact you? Make it easy by having contact information on your media/press page. This can simply be an email or form for people to fill out. It can go directly to your assistant, your publicist, or a generic email. Remember to always simplify and make it as easy as possible for someone to look you up, see what you're about, and get a hold of you.

## FOR BUSINESS OWNERS AND NONPROFITS

This is a great place to include a brief company history, a mission statement, and values, along with any awards that you have received. These are all important pieces that a journalist or host might want to refer to. If you've achieved some major fundraising goals and/or have press release materials around such a thing, this is a great place to house that information as well.

## FOR AUTHORS

If you've written a book, then you should provide graphics to download your book cover (front AND back) along with a summary/description of the book, links to where it can be purchased, your author bio, book endorsements, title, subtitle, publisher, publishing date, ISBN number, number of pages, and a short excerpt.

## FOR POLITICAL CANDIDATES, ADVOCATES, AND ACTIVISTS

Your media/press page is a great place to include your endorsements, recognizable names that agree with your advocacy, awards or causes you've championed, your bio, and your reason "why," along with your headshots, interviews, and features.

In every example, it might seem like your media/press page includes a number of components that your website also has pages for, such as your About page. The reason for this is because your media/press page stands as the place where a host can glean all the information about you and your book, organization, business, or cause in order to make a decision on interviewing you, as well as where to gather the information needed for an interview or feature. This is a condensed version of your website where you offer instant downloads of preapproved content (your headshot, logo, book cover, and so on).

## YOUR MEDIA/PRESS PAGE IS A BENEFIT TO OTHERS

Your media/press page isn't just a benefit for you to showcase who you are and where you've been featured. It's also not just a place for a host or journalist to visit and gather info or make a decision on whether or not to interview you. There's a HUGE benefit to the hosts of podcasts that have interviewed you. In Chapter 6, I shared how promoting your interviews not only is an important part of thanking a host but is a "must" in my book. Having your interview with a link to the actual episode will create more downloads of the episode, which is essentially what every podcaster is striving for.

I briefly touched on backlinks earlier and how they can be beneficial. They ultimately link one website to another. By linking directly to your podcast interviews, you're creating a backlink for the podcast host. A backlink creates web traffic to the website you are linking to. Whether or not you are familiar with websites or podcasts, you certainly know that website owners and podcast hosts want to drive more traffic to their sites and shows. The more listeners, readers, and followers a person can get, the more beneficial it is for the person. The benefits of reaching a greater audience can include attracting sponsors for content (show me the $$$!), attracting advertisers, getting increased audience engagement that can lead to new clients and more business, garnering a larger following that can help propel a book proposal, being offered speaking engagements, and much more. The impact that you can have by sharing a link from one website to yours is pretty incredible and means that the impact you are creating with your message just got that much bigger!

I want to point out that this benefit isn't just one that is for the podcast host. The majority of hosts are offering you the exact same benefit with the show notes they provide for your interview. Remember in Chapter 7 how I shared that repurposing your interview into your own show notes had links included in the template example? The podcast host has already done this on his or her own website AND included the links you provided to the host. The links you supply are up to you, but they should include your website, your social media handles, a link to your freebie (which asks for an email address in return!), and anything else you might be mentioning in the interview, such as where people can buy your new book. You are now the lucky recipient of backlinks to your own website from the podcast host's website! It's a win-win, as most podcast interviews are!

## WHAT'S THE HOST UP TO . . . PROMOTION, PROMOTION, PROMOTION!

Podcast hosts are ALWAYS busy promoting their podcast . . . or at least they should be! Hosts who know good marketing practices understand the importance of promotion and sharing more than once and on more than one platform. While you are adding your latest interview to your media/press page, hosts are promoting their weekly episode on every podcast listening platform (Apple, Google, Spotify, iHeart, Audible, Amazon, Player FM, Pocket Casts, Stitcher, Podbean, Castbox, TuneIn, YouTube, and more). In addition to the audio file they've uploaded everywhere, they've created graphics for social media and captions to post on Instagram, Facebook, X, TikTok, Pinterest, LinkedIn, and others.

Besides using social media, hosts are promoting their episodes on their website with show notes, podcast players, graphics, and links. Many podcast hosts also have email lists that they are growing. Weekly emails are sent summarizing their episodes so that their subscribers don't miss a single one.

Many hosts will revisit episodes within their current episode to link back to them or post on social media a reminder to check out a certain episode. Promotion doesn't simply happen on the day an episode goes live; it should be continually happening and distributed in multiple places.

---

## EXERCISE

### Create Your Media/Press Page

It's time for you to create a media/press page on your website! Add a new page to your website along with including it as an option from your header menu for visitors to click on. The name can be interchangeable, so select the one you prefer: "Media Page" or "Press Page." Before you add your previous interviews (or even before you've booked an interview), add the following items to your page:

- Approved headshots (don't forget to give credit to your photographer)
- Long bio
- Short bio
- Company description (if you have one)
- Causes you have championed/elections won (if applicable)
- Awards won (if applicable)
- Book cover graphic (if applicable)
- Summary of your book (if applicable)
- Contact information to book you
- Downloadable logos
- Downloadable media kit
- Speaking topics

Next, add images for the interviews you've done. Remember that this can be a generic graphic icon, such as a microphone, or it can be the podcast cover art or logo of the outlet. Hyperlink the image to your interview, and add the title of the interview under the image/graphic/logo.

## SUMMARY

Your media/press page is a podcast host's one-stop shop to gather all the information the host needs on you . . . who you are, what your company or book is about, your headshots, your topics, and where you've been featured. You've made it easy for someone to learn all there is to know about you! Way to go!

Don't forget to keep this page updated. Since you are already utilizing a Trello board to keep track of your pitches and interviews, there's a line under "Checklist" for you to remember to add it to your media/press page! By updating your page with every interview, it won't become overwhelming when you suddenly have 10 or more to update . . . because you are going to have a lot of interviews to add to your media/press page!

# THE WORLD IS WAITING FOR YOUR INTERVIEWS

## YOU HAVE WHAT IT TAKES TO PITCH YOURSELF AND BE AN INCREDIBLE GUEST, SO GO DO IT!

## A QUICK RECAP

Friend, our journey is coming to an end, and yet this is just the beginning for you. I have done my very best to ensure that you have all the tips and tools from my podcast pitching toolkit to make you successful in not only landing podcast interviews but also maximizing the way you utilize them after the recording has stopped.

You are an expert. You have a message. You have a story. You have a cause. You have a business. You have a book. Whatever it is that you have, the world is waiting to hear about it. The world needs to know you and all that you bring to the table. It's YOUR job to share that knowledge because there's no one who can do it like you do.

We've uncovered your unique speaking topics, which is one of the most important parts in this book. It's truly the thing that sets you apart from everyone else in your field and in life. It highlights your expertise and truly defines who you are, what you know, what you stand for, and what you've been through. You've been able to take those topics and create a beautifully branded media kit to share with podcast hosts that highlights what you speak on and gives hosts a complete view of who you are, what your expertise is, and what you love to talk about. Not only do they get this from your media kit, but the branding of your media kit will also entice a certain emotion or feeling in them based on the colors and fonts you use, just as your website does.

As you research podcasts, make sure you connect with the host and the podcast. You'll be able to do this by listening to an episode or two and checking out the host's website and social media platforms. This sounds like a lot of extra work, and it does take some time. BUT it is worth it, and I hope you've learned this important lesson throughout this book. Hosts will immediately recognize the extra steps and care you've taken to find out who they are and what their show is about. Adding in details that you've found about them is going to make your pitch stand out from every other pitch they receive. I promise you that much . . . because I'm a fellow stalker and know it works! Being thoughtful in your pitch and showing that you aren't simply pitching yourself for selfish reasons but to help the hosts and their audience is going to take your pitch from good to great. One of the biggest compliments I receive is on my pitches because they aren't copy and paste. They're unique to every host I email. If you only learn one thing, please know that there is no copy and paste in pitching!

Don't worry if you get butterflies going into your first interview. You are the expert. You know your story and your message and that what you have to say is important. It will get easier as you get more interviews under your belt, but know that some butterflies can also be a good thing. They show that you care about what you're doing. If you do your homework, and I know you will, then you will show up prepared and record an expert interview every single time. Remember that practice makes perfect!

Thank your hosts, and remember the importance of going the extra mile by sharing with them and tagging them—and remember that doing so for more than a 24-hour period of time is what is the most beneficial, both for you and for the host. Create templates and processes for you and your team to follow so that when an interview goes live, it's absolute plug-and-play and requires the bare minimum amount of work to get it out there on all your platforms and website. There are ways to make all of this easy, and it just takes some organization and strategy before you start. Spend that extra time beforehand so that you aren't left scrambling and in disarray with a bunch of interviews down the road that haven't been shared or posted.

## JUST START

If you've been doing the work as you've been reading, then you are more than ready to go. If you've just finished reading this book and are thinking this is a lot of work, I want to encourage you to just start. Start doing the work, because if you don't, no one is going to do it for you. You aren't going to become visible or discovered by sitting back and continuing to do whatever it is you do on a daily basis. How do I know? Well, has it happened so far?

## NOT JUST YOUR STORY—YOUR LEGACY

I believe every human being has something to share, something that others can learn from, and it's up to each and every one of us to share that. This isn't just about sharing your knowledge or changing lives though. It's about creating and leaving your legacy for others. While you've been busy contemplating how podcast interviews are going to grow your business, advocate for your cause, gain new voters, sell your book, and create a thought leader out of you, there's one thing I'm sure you haven't quite considered. What will it be like for your family and future generations to be able to hear from you? Your own voice, your message, your experience, and your story.

Your voice is powerful, and the ability to have it live on long after you're gone has to be one of the most compelling reasons for recording podcast interviews. This is something I consider every time I hit

"Record" on my own show. Not only am I creating content for followers and to build my business, but I'm also recording my opinion and views on what is going on in the world for my children to listen to one day. They'll never have to wonder what their mom would think of a certain topic because it's all recorded . . . in my own voice and in my own words. This is the power of a podcast. This is the power YOU now have access to.

## USING PODCAST INTERVIEWS TO POWER YOUR MARKETING PLAN

Podcast pitching and interviews are a form of earned public relations, but they're also key ingredients in powering your marketing plan. You can easily AND simply create marketing content for all your social media platforms and website in multiple ways with just one podcast interview. You've just learned how to create unique speaking topics and how to create a beautifully branded media kit along with finding podcasts that align with your message and audience. You've learned how to authentically pitch to hosts and their audience, how to be a podcast guest who will long be remembered, and how to be grateful for what you've received from your host. And what's more, you've also walked away armed with at least 12 different ways to repurpose every single one of your interviews. From one interview you can create a post for the overall episode and multiple posts for various quotes for that episode—that's over a week's worth of content for one platform. Spread that over other platforms, and you now have a minimum of 20 pieces of content . . . in other words, one podcast interview just gave you an entire month's worth of social media content. I have yet to see a platform, let alone an entire book, that will help you do this!

Use this golden nugget of a toolkit to your advantage. As an entrepreneur, I understand and know how much time we dedicate to creating valuable content. I get how it can become dreadful to think about because of the time and effort it can take . . . so let's change our way of thinking by repurposing our podcast interviews. You're going to find not only that your visibility and sales increase, but that your stress and anxiety over having so much to do is going to actually decrease as well.

Do your part . . . go pitch yourself and share yourself with the world. I'm cheering you on and will also share the interviews you land (tag me on social media, so I see them!). I'm so very proud of you for starting this journey and growing as a business owner, author, and advocate and, most importantly, as a human being. You were put on this earth for a reason, so now it's time to share that with the world!

# ACKNOWLEDGMENTS

I'm humbled every day by the fact that my clients have chosen me to help them tell their stories. I'm grateful to every single one of them and to every podcast host who has said yes to my pitches and helped change the world, one voice at a time. Thank you for putting your trust in me.

Thank you to my book coach, Gretel Hakanson, who was the first person I worked with on the journey to bringing this book to life. She never questioned my insistence on getting everything done ahead of deadlines and gave me the right balance of push and gentleness.

I'm grateful to my agents, Jacquie Flynn and Joelle Delbourgo, for believing this book deserved a home and for finding it the perfect home with McGraw Hill. Thank you for being in my corner and looking out for me.

To my former editor, Michele Matrisciani, I am so thankful that my book fell into your hands and for your immense belief that the world needed it. I knew you were the perfect person to work with from the moment we had our first Zoom call. Thank you for believing in me.

Thank you to Christopher Brown, Jonanthan Sperling, and the entire McGraw Hill team for all your hard work on my book. McGraw

Hill has felt like home for me and my book, and I appreciate each and every one of you for making my dream become a reality.

I can't not include the two artists who got me through writing this entire book. Although they most likely will never read this, a BIG thank you to Harry Styles and Jeremy Renner. I had you both on repeat while writing this book and am grateful to you not only for your songs, but also because you both represent inspiration to myself and others.

To my friends who have supported me on this journey from the very beginning. Thank you Keren de Zwart for believing in me and pushing me to keep going, even when I doubted things. I am beyond words at how lucky I am to call you friend and to have you in my corner. Thank you Merle R. Saferstein for your friendship and love. You are a true gift to the world and I'm so grateful to call you friend and to have learned what living a legacy means from you. Thank you for always cheering me on and being a listening ear. Thank you Leigh Stein for always answering my crazy questions and reminding me that it's all going to be OK. I'm lucky that I could slide into your DMs and we have created a friendship across the country. Thank you Allison Stephanian for being the mom friend and teammate I've needed. Thank you for always saying yes when I've asked for help and celebrating with me. Thank you to my neighbor and mom friend, Nahal Nabavi. I'm so grateful for our backyard gate chats, your supportive friendship, and for encouraging me to use my voice and speak up. I love that our kids have each other to play with and make memories together from their backyards! Thank you to my therapist, Lisa Eaton, who has been the voice of not only reason, but encouragement over the years.

Thank you to my Happy Hour Crew! Cindy (and Mike), Sara (and Terry), and Jill (and Rob) for not only supporting me, but for being there for my family. We are so lucky to have you as our chosen aunts and uncles for our kids! Thank you for never questioning my text messages in need of an emergency happy hour and dropping everything to be here, whether it's to celebrate or commiserate.

A huge thank you to my tiny humans, Declan and Katharine. The cheerleading, support, hugs, and love you show me on a daily basis are absolute gifts. You both are such a blessing and I'm so proud to be your mom. Thank you for letting me finish typing my thoughts before asking for another snack and for telling all your friends and even strangers that I've written a book. I love and adore you both more than you'll ever know.

Last, but most certainly not least, thank you to my husband, partner, and best friend, Ted. You have supported me throughout this journey and all the pivots along the way, and I'm eternally grateful. Thank you for listening, for giving me your advice, for helping me find the right synonyms, for pouring me another glass of wine, and for celebrating with me. We make a great team and there's no one else I'd rather be with on this journey of life. Thank you for loving me, encouraging me to use my voice and go after my dreams, and for always trusting me in my decisions, no matter how quickly I make them. I love you, Ted.

# INDEX

X (formerly Twitter), repurposing
content for, 148

*You, Me, and Anxiety* (Graham), 37
*Your Fully Charged Life* (Murphy),
112

YouTube videos, 97, 104

Zencastr, 94
Zoom, 93–94, 97

# ABOUT THE AUTHOR

**Michelle Glogovac** (San Jose, California), aka The Podcast Matchmaker™, is an award-winning podcast publicist and host of the *My Simplified Life* podcast. She matches her clients with the perfect podcast hosts and teaches them how to share their story, vision, and expertise in ways that generate new business opportunities. Michelle speaks on a variety of topics, including PR, entrepreneurship, and life lessons and has interviewed and worked with Emmy Award winners, international bestselling authors, advocates and activists, and many other individuals. She is the founder and CEO of The MLG Collective®, a podcast public relations agency.

Please visit her website at www.michelleglogovac.com.

Please find her on Instagram at @michelleglogovac.